Emily Brontë

Editors:
Linda Cookson
Bryan Loughrey

Editors: Linda Cookson and Bryan Loughrey

Titles in the series:

CONTENTS

PREFACE

Like all professional groups, literary critics have developed their own specialised language. This is not necessarily a bad thing. Sometimes complex concepts can only be described in a terminology far removed from everyday speech. Academic jargon, however, creates an unnecessary barrier between the critic and the intelligent but less practised reader.

This danger is particularly acute where scholarly books and articles are re-packaged for a student audience. Critical anthologies, for example, often contain extracts from longer studies originally written for specialists. Deprived of their original context, these passages can puzzle and at times mislead. The essays in this volume, however, are all specially commissioned, self-contained works, written with the needs of students firmly in mind.

This is not to say that the contributors — all experienced critics and teachers — have in any way attempted to simplify the complexity of the issues with which they deal. On the contrary, they explore the central problems of the text from a variety of critical perspectives, reaching conclusions which are challenging and at times mutually contradictory.

They try, however, to present their arguments in a direct, accessible language and to work within the limitations of scope and length which students inevitably face. For this reason, essays are generally rather briefer than is the practice; they address quite specific topics; and, in line with examination requirements, they incorporate precise textual detail into the body of the discussion.

They offer, therefore, working examples of the kind of essay-writing skills which students themselves are expected to develop. Their diversity, however, should act as a reminder that in the field of literary studies there is no such thing as a 'model' answer. Good essays are the outcome of a creative engagement with literature, of sensitive, attentive reading and careful thought. We hope that those contained in this volume will encourage students to return to the most important starting point of all, the text itself, with renewed excitement and the determination to explore more fully their own critical responses.

How to use this volume

Obviously enough, you should start by reading the text in question. The one assumption that all the contributors make is that you are already familiar with this. It would be helpful, of course, to have read further — perhaps other works by the same author or by influential contemporaries. But we don't assume that you have yet had the opportunity to do this and any references to historical background or to other works of literature are explained.

You should, perhaps, have a few things to hand. It is always a good idea to keep a copy of the text nearby when reading critical studies. You will almost certainly want to consult it when checking the context of quotations or pausing to consider the validity of the critic's interpretation. You should also try to have access to a good dictionary, and ideally a copy of a dictionary of literary terms as well. The contributors have tried to avoid jargon and to express themselves clearly and directly. But inevitably there will be occasional words or phrases with which you are unfamiliar. Finally, we would encourage you to make notes, summarising not just the argument of each essay but also your own responses to what you have read. So keep a pencil and notebook at the ready.

Suitably equipped, the best thing to do is simply begin with whichever topic most interests you. We have deliberately organised each volume so that the essays may be read in any order. One consequence of this is that, for the sake of clarity and self-containment, there is occasionally a degree of overlap between essays. But at least you are not forced to follow one — fairly arbitrary — reading sequence.

Each essay is followed by brief 'Afterthoughts', designed to highlight points of critical interest. But remember, these are only there to remind you that it is *your* responsibility to question what you read. The essays printed here are not a series of 'model' answers to be slavishly imitated and in no way should they be regarded as anything other than a guide or stimulus for your own thinking. We hope for a critically involved response: 'That was interesting. But if *I* were tackling the topic . . .!'

Read the essays in this spirit and you'll pick up many of the skills of critical composition in the process. We have, however, tried to provide more explicit advice in 'A practical guide to essay writing'. You may find this helpful, but do not imagine it offers any magic formulas. The quality of your essays ultimately depends on the quality of your engagement with literary texts. We hope this volume spurs you on to read these with greater understanding and to explore your responses in greater depth.

Paul Norgate

Paul Norgate has taught English in a variety of educational establishments, and is the author of several critical studies.

ESSAY

The almanack and the window: narrative, time and viewpoint in the structure of *Wuthering Heights*

It is easy to find words such as 'powerful' and 'intense' to describe the impact of *Wuthering Heights*; not quite so simple to explain precisely the source of that power and intensity. It is easy to recall from the novel relationships of extraordinary passion, incidents of extraordinary violence; but in retracing our steps to dwell over these, we are likely to find ourselves reminded also that a great deal of the novel appears to be concerned with matters of an almost extreme ordinariness. Much that is put before our attention as we read seems to bear little direct relevance to the relationship of Heathliff and Cathy and its consequences — that is, to what most readers would see as the crux of the novel. How, then, might we account for these apparent contradictions? What is the relationship of intensity to ordinariness in the novel? What connections can be made between the structure and the effects of *Wuthering Heights*?

To trace connections — between events, characters, themes,

novel of opposites.
mean a play of opposites:
B+B vs. C+H

images, or whatever — within a text, is to attempt to uncover the ways it holds together and generates 'meaning'. In *Wuthering Heights* we encounter a novel which at first seems quite deliberately to draw attention to its own patterns of organisation. The opening word of the novel is a date — '1801'; the second — 'I' — introduces a narrator. As the novel proceeds, we are repeatedly made aware of how the story-telling shifts from one person to another, and of the shifts and passage of time in and between their narratives. Meanwhile the story of the central characters takes shape in a complex collage of recollection and reflection, conversation and correspondence, diary and dream.

Despite its apparent openness and 'innocence', however, there are several aspects of the novel's structure which may strike us as somewhat unexpected. We are, for instance, accustomed generally to stories which are told from a consistent viewpoint — that either of the 'omniscient' author, who can tell us everything about everything, or of a single 'I' who is a character with a significant place in or outlook on the action. In *Wuthering Heights* the way the text is organised seems repeatedly to require that we pay attention first to the peripheral figures of Lockwood and Nelly, often through an accumulation of commonplace and seemingly irrelevant detail. (Lockwood relates how he insisted that Nelly should stay up late to tell him the story of Heathcliff; we hear the minutiae of their discussion on what constitutes a decent bedtime; Lockwood insists on making links between the progress of his illness and that of Nelly's narrative; Nelly produces and reads aloud the actual letter written by Isabella describing her arrival at the Heights; and so on.)

Then there is the continual interruption and fragmentation of ordered chronological sequence, brought about by the multiplicity of narrators and their different methods and moments of narration. It is certainly possible to construct from the novel, in retrospect, a meticulously detailed calendar of events; but it should be stressed that this is not what we are most aware of as we are actually reading. Periods of sustained intensity alternate with sudden shifts and gaps, and our sense of a steady passage of time in the narrative (for instance, as children grow up) is minimal; events in Nelly's telling are 'shot direct' at us, rather after the fashion of Isabella's bounding, leaping flight from the Heights (chapter 17). What is more, those dates which the novel offers as 'landmarks' (1801 and 1802 — chapter 1, chapter 32) turn out to be apparently arbitrary, relating only to Lockwood's preoccupation with his own comings and goings. We notice that none of the crucial events involving the central characters is presented to us directly or immediately; five of the eight main characters in the novel are in fact already dead before Lockwood opens his journal. No sooner have we tracked through this narrative maze back to the 'present' (the winter of 1801–1802; chapter 1, chapter 30) than the pattern eludes us again, as the novel leaps several months ahead to set off a further sequence of 'flashback'. Even the death of Heathcliff and the reconciliation of Catherine and Hareton — events which occur during Lockwood's tenancy of the Grange — are held as it were at a distance, framed (like almost everything else) in the reported narrative of Nelly.

The structure of *Wuthering Heights*, then, might appear at first almost deliberately perverse. Continually it draws our attention to the trivial, the ordinary and the irrelevant, even as we are aware of the profound, the extraordinary and the compelling taking shape within it. The 'frame', we might say, threatens to obscure the picture. But what happens if we take away the frame? To pension off the narrators and straighten out the time scheme might tumble us more quickly into the 'main' plot, but it's doubtful whether we should then make any more sense of what would be left in the novel — or even be prepared to bother with it at all. It has often been pointed out how a summary of the plot proves totally inadequate to the effect of the novel as a whole, the extreme and frequently violent incidents reducing to a catalogue of melodrama and sensationalism.

So we must conclude that the narrative structure in *Wuthering Heights* — the constant movement between contrasting alternatives of extremity and ordinariness — is in fact not merely perverse, a surface (dis)organisation that gets in the way of the 'real' story. I'd like to suggest that this movement should itself be seen as a part of the story — or, more accurately, of the way we make sense of the story. On the one hand, the very violence and intensity of the central events causes fragmentation and radical disorder in the telling of them: Heathcliff's 'monomania', as Nelly terms it, demands a multiplicity of narrators;

it provokes from others, whose lives run on a different level, repeated and overlapping attempts at a task of comprehension to which none of them individually is adequate. At the same time, the intricate ordinariness within which events and characters are gradually pieced together, the mosaic of dates and narrators, provides a familiar and manageable context; a means by which we can begin to grasp the scale, and gain access to the significance, of what is going on.

Let us attempt to trace something of this interplay of opposites through just one episode of the novel. In chapter 9 of *Wuthering Heights* there occurs a decisive turning point when Heathcliff, having overheard Cathy say that 'it would degrade me to marry Heathcliff now', leaves the Heights and is seen no more for three years. This is the climax of a sequence in the novel so packed with incident (Cathy hits Edgar Linton; Hindley threatens Nelly and then drops the infant Hareton over the banister; Cathy bursts out passionately that 'Nelly, I *am* Heathcliff!') that it is difficult at first to isolate or recall any single reason for Heathcliff's departure. On inspection, however, the trail leads back to a dispute between Cathy and Heathcliff, in chapter 8:

> '. . . only look at the almanack, on that wall.' He pointed to a framed sheet hanging near the window, and continued: 'The crosses are for the evenings you have spent with the Lintons, the dots for those spent with me. Do you see? I've marked every day.'

The actual argument is brief, and is soon interrupted by the arrival of its ostensible cause, Edgar Linton. What really sparks it off, though, is Heathcliff's reference to the almanack.

There is an obvious contrast here between the triviality which triggers the dispute, and its far-reaching consequences. Unexpected as it may seem to find Heathcliff joining the tribe of the Lockwoods and Nellies in his reliance on the almanack, we should note exactly what is happening. Forced, as has never before been necessary, to try and articulate the strength of his feelings for Cathy — and hence of his resentment now at her apparent betrayal of him — Heathcliff can find no way of beginning, except with the 'proof' he has doggedly, bitterly recorded on the almanack. This persistent, absolute detail of dots and

crosses, which so infuriates Cathy, represents the onl
Heathcliff can express himself with anything like t'
ness he intends. (Here, in fact, is a clue to understanᴅᵢₙg
of his later behaviour — including the enormity of his revenge,
which in its utter, enduring thoroughness simply pursues to its
ultimate conclusion the same principle as his marking of the
almanack.)

Cathy, on the other hand, refuses to countenance this
literal-minded way of seeing things:

> '. . . very foolish; as if I took notice! . . . where is the sense of
> that?'

(chapter 8)

Time is simply irrelevant to the way in which she conceives of
the relationship between herself and Heathcliff, as she explains
to Nelly shortly afterwards:

> 'My love for Linton is like the foliage in the woods. Time will
> change it . . . My love for Heathcliff resembles the eternal rocks
> beneath . . . Nelly, I *am* Heathcliff — he's always, always in my
> mind . . .'

(chapter 9)

'Foliage' as against 'rocks'; Cathy is quite sure of herself in the
way she contrasts her feelings for the two men, although she
seems not to appreciate that things may be less clear to Heathcliff. Picking up again the argument over the almanack, we are
able to compare Cathy's words with Heathcliff's actual
interpretation of her feelings for him; again there is a contrast,
similar to that of 'foliage' and 'rocks', but this time it is one
which runs directly counter to Cathy's certainty. Instead of her
'eternal rocks beneath', Heathcliff identifies her feelings with
the leaves of the almanack, speckled with dots and crosses.
Ironies and contradictions abound, as might be expected when
contrasting alternatives are forced into such intense relationship as here. No sooner has Cathy insisted to Nelly that Heathcliff is 'always, always in my mind' than we see time already
at work, undermining her words: Heathcliff, overhearing that
'it would degrade me to marry Heathcliff now' (chapter 9), does
not stay the few short minutes longer which would have enabled
him also to hear her passionate explanation. For the next three

years, the only place Heathcliff can be for Cathy is in her mind.
In turn Heathcliff, who in his demand for time with Cathy has
been counting days on the almanack, promptly 'loses' three
whole years of his life, and in effect loses Cathy for ever.

The argument between Heathcliff and Cathy in chapter 8
is clearly important at levels well beyond the immediate issue
of 'who were you with last night?' At stake is the significance
of time itself in people's lives. On the one hand (we might say),
as human beings time is all we have, and therefore time is
everything. If Cathy gives herself — her time — to someone
else, Heathcliff is lost and his life is empty; the only purposeful
way for him then to fill his time is in taking revenge on those
who prevent their being together. Yet from a different, perhaps
more imaginative viewpoint, the mapping out of time is arti-
ficial and ultimately irrelevant: 'What were the use of my
creation if I were entirely contained here?' asks Cathy (chapter
9). For her, time and the actions it contains and defines hardly
count at all, by contrast with her own inner feelings, and the
arguments against her supposed conduct put forward here by
Heathcliff (and later by Nelly and Edgar) are not really arguments at all; they miss the point.

Emerging from the clash of views between Heathcliff and
Cathy can be seen again the pattern of contrasting alternatives:
against the man-made organisation of the almanack are set the
'eternal rocks beneath'; against the literal-minded marking-off
of dots and crosses, the imaginative inclusiveness of 'always,
always'. In the flaring-up of this adolescent dispute over the
almanack we are suddenly aware, through Heathcliff and
Cathy, of the structural pattern of the novel finding expression
in the characters themselves. Their argument forces them into
the expression of two opposing attitudes to experience, two
alternative ways of seeing life. Yet at the same time the force
of attraction between Heathcliff and Cathy is unbroken; if
anything, the barriers of argument and subsequent separation
make it the more intense — and, ultimately, destructive.

When Heathcliff returns (chapter 10), Cathy attempts to act
as if nothing has changed — consistent with her declaration on
the day of his departure: 'He'll be as much to me as he has been
all his lifetime' (chapter 9). Yet for Heathcliff, of course, everything appears irretrievably altered. Cathy is married to Edgar,

has moved to Thrushcross Grange and (as becomes apparent shortly) is now pregnant. The almanack is crowded with events marking ways in which he has been betrayed. He plans a revenge that will occupy his time until death. Cathy responds with her ultimate attempt to break out of the limitations of time, willing her own death. 'I shall be incomparably above and beyond you all,' she cries. (chapter 15). But Heathcliff is unable to escape 'beyond' time; '*do* not leave me in this abyss, where I cannot find you!' he cries, after her death (chapter 16). He remains trapped, held in, while she escapes into death.

Entrapment and escape, holding in and opening out: these contrasting impulses and the conflicting energies they generate are at work continually (and often violently) in and around the story of Heathcliff and Cathy. Our earliest glimpse of the pair is of their breaking out from childhood imprisonment at the Heights, as recorded in Cathy's diary which Lockwood discovers in the margins of 'Seventy Times Seven'. When, in his temporary sanctuary in the innermost enclosure of the Heights, the closet bed, Lockwood first opens the book and then breaks open the 'soldered' window to let in storm, fear and the ghost, the intensity of those energies finds shocking expression in the 'civilised' man's imagined violence to the ghostly child: 'I pulled its wrist on to the broken pane, and rubbed it to and fro until the blood ran down . . .' (chapter 3).

As conflict and contrast repeatedly burst out in the plot and break into the narrative, so their potential is repeatedly signalled even in the smallest details of the text itself. The almanack episode again provides an illustration. At the very moment when the crucial argument begins in the kitchen at Wuthering Heights, our attention is directed (almost in passing) to the almanack and the window: 'He pointed to a framed sheet hanging near the window' (chapter 8). A commonplace comment would be that their presence helps 'bring the scene to life', but — given that we are not just collecting random 'documentary' details about farmhouse life in eighteenth-century Yorkshire — the almanack and the window are more than incidental features on the wall of the plot. No matter how briefly, they are marked out as something specific, elements in the developing structure of the novel.

The almanack on the wall, we notice, is 'framed' — and so

held in, contained, fixed — but it is 'hanging near the window', which opens out onto the wild moorland that offers repeated opportunities of 'escape' in the course of the novel. These are details, then, which certainly 'bring things to life' — but not just in terms of a setting or a period. Directing our attention to the constant possibility of contrast, of alternative ways of seeing things, the almanack and the window are parts of our experience of the novel which help us to make sense of the *whole*. They are details which — in combination with a myriad others — signal the movement of powerful and conflicting energies which run, not just in the one brief argument, but throughout the novel.

Analysis of the almanack episode suggests that an interplay of contrasting alternatives characterises the structure of *Wuthering Heights* at all levels, from apparently minor 'descriptive' details to the continual movement of viewpoint and chronology in the narrative itself. In such a structural pattern, none of the extremes or alternatives contained within it can be seen as complete in itself or exclusively 'right'. The structure of *Wuthering Heights* in short, denies us any fixed point from which to judge what is going on within it. The only thing that is definite is that nothing is definite.

In the absence of an omniscient author/narrator, we are continually reminded how everything we read is subjective — conditioned by the attitudes, preconceptions, limitations, or plain bias, of narrators whose only existence is within the conflicts of the text itself. None of them can be totally objective, none can be the ultimate judge of everything that goes on. As Nelly herself points out: 'you'll judge as well as I can, all these things; at least, you'll think you will, and that's the same (chapter 17). As the novel unfolds, we find ourselves sympathising, in turn, with radically conflicting viewpoints: Lockwood, then Heathcliff; Hindley, then Nelly; Cathy, then Edgar. At other points and in different circumstances each of these same viewpoints may appear to us quite inadequate, or even totally repellent. By the end of the novel we should have learned, at the very least, not to take anything for granted. How complete — how accurate — is, for instance, Lockwood's final impression (chapter 34) of a 'benign sky' and the impossibility of 'unquiet slumbers, for the sleepers in that quiet earth'? Does Nelly's account to Lockwood reveal on her part any greater penetration or insight into her subjects now, in retrospect, than did her responses (as she reports them) at the time — or than do Lockwood's own formulations and reformulations of opinion in the 'present'?

The partial and mistaken judgements passed on to us by the various narrators reflect what happens within the narrative itself, as characters attempt to come to terms with each other and their circumstances. Lockwood speculates fatuously on the marriageability of the younger Catherine, while simultaneously depicting to us her blind scorning of the unfortunate Hareton (chapter 31). Narrators relate, one after another, their encounters with life at the Heights. All, to a greater or lesser extent, come to it as 'outsiders' (as, by way of variation, does Heathcliff to the Grange): how far does any of them adequately grasp or respond to what is going on there, as distinct from their own expectations or illusions?

All such judgements and misjudgements are generated, as we have noted, within the text; they are expressed through fictional figures in whom are established certain points of view or attitudes. But to the extent that any attitude or outlook on life is established or 'fixed', so — no matter how 'ordinary' or 'normal' it appears — unwittingly it identifies itself as a kind of extreme. In making the assumption of its own rightness or normality, it will in turn inevitably resist as 'extreme' whatever seems unfamiliar, different and therefore threatening. 'Extremes' in this way generate and perpetuate each other, and once we perceive how it works, examples of this process begin to multiply in the novel. For instance (as hinted earlier), we need to ask in what ways the extremity of Heathcliff is 'real', and how far it is 'created' — either by other characters (Hindley? Cathy?), in their treatment of him, or by those who narrate him (are not the urbane sophistication of Lockwood and Nelly's relentless conventionality also, in their own ways, extremes?). Cathy's behaviour, when she locks herself in and starves herself (chapters 11–12), may be called extreme; but is there not some justice in her sense of incredulity at Edgar's ability to sit and read in his library — at his equally 'extreme' behaviour?

I suggested earlier that the unusual narrative structure of *Wuthering Heights*, with its fragmented viewpoints and disrupted chronology, might be explained as a consequence of the 'extremity' of what it contains. Perhaps it would be more accurate to conclude that the true source of the novel's intensity lies in the narrative structure itself, as much as in any 'episode' or 'character' we may isolate within it. The power of *Wuthering Heights* is not — as is sometimes implied — a marvellous mystery, explicable only in terms of the darker recesses of the romantic imagination. It is a power generated — in ways and at points which are identifiable — within the actual text, through patterns of continual movement and contrast; and by the constant interplay (to which the novel itself draws attention) of narrative, time and viewpoint in its structure.

AFTERTHOUGHTS

1

What 'unexpected' aspects of the novel's structure are identified in this essay (pages 10–11)?

2

What significance does Norgate attach to Heathcliff's reference to the almanack in chapter 8 (page 12)?

3

What relationship does Norgate see between the ordinary and the extraordinary in *Wuthering Heights*?

4

What are the advantages of having several narrators in *Wuthering Heights*?

Claire Saunders

Claire Saunders teaches English at Lavant House and has extensive experience as an A-level English Literature examiner.

[handwritten: moors vs. buildings → freedom, acceptance → imprisonment rules]

ESSAY

Place in *Wuthering Heights*

A tall, dark, handsome man locked in a passionate embrace with a beautiful, wild-looking girl — this could be the cover-picture for a thousand romantic novels. But set those figures against craggy moorland scenery and they are immediately identifiable as Heathcliff and Catherine in *Wuthering Heights*. The image is so strong, so instantly recognisable, that it has come to denote Emily Brontë's lovers (just as a man in black contemplating a skull denotes Hamlet). The scene is a classic, perfect material for exploitation in comic sketches, charades, even television advertisements. Actually there is no such scene in the novel. The crucial element in the popular image is the strong dramatic background which seems to reflect the strong dramatic love of the story, all captured in the name — *Wuthering Heights*. Brontë's choice of title — instead of the expected 'Heathcliff', perhaps — suggests that, as in Austen's *Mansfield Park* or Eliot's *Middlemarch*, the place is more than just a setting for the story. *[handwritten: Becomes a character in its own right?]*

In real life or 'realistic' films the setting in which human beings are observed may well be insignificant — since people cannot realistically be shown nowhere, their background may be merely the medium in which they exist, necessary but neutral. In a novel, however, where characters are people made of words, place is only necessary when the novelist wants it to be; every detail of the setting is, therefore, a positive element of the novel, significant to the reader. The novelist, like a painter, decides what we are to see. But this analogy is too simple in that the novelist's scene is not a single, stable canvas. Firstly the dimension of time in a novel means that any place may be modified by change — by weather, time of day, the passing months or years. Secondly, the point of view can be multiple or shifting as the novelist allows a place to be seen from varying angles, with varying definition or focus, according to the different perceptions of the characters or narrators. *Wuthering Heights*, with its span of two generations and its multiple narrators, is particularly rich and complex in the depiction of place. The physical scope is very limited; within a few square miles of moorland are two houses; the outward action is set within a few rooms and the immediate environs of these two houses; the inward action focuses even more narrowly — on two small spaces, the bed and the grave. But these few elements of the setting are used with subtle intensity, serving the plot, revealing characters and embodying the emotions and ideas at the heart of the novel.

At the simplest level Wuthering Heights is a property, something to be owned, a sign of status. We are introduced to Wuthering Heights as 'the name of Mr Heathcliff's dwelling', yet over the main door is carved 'Hareton Earnshaw'. The plot of the novel could be seen as tracing the hows and whys of the changing fortunes of the house; Hindley Earnshaw inherits it from the line of Earnshaws going back to 1500; Heathcliff wins it as his revenge against Hindley; fate and patience return it eventually to Hindley's son. But this Hareton will desert it. The malevolent Joseph will live on in the kitchen but the rest of Wuthering Heights will be 'shut up' for ever. A desolate tale, yet seeming appropriate to our original view of the house and its forbidding name.

Wuthering Heights was named after its position, the adjective being 'descriptive of the atmospheric tumult to which its station is exposed in stormy weather' (chapter 1). It is set high up, the harsh, shelterless location eloquently expressed in the vegetation:

One may guess the power of the north wind blowing over the

edge, by the excessive slant of a few stunted firs at the end of the house; and by a range of gaunt thorns all stretching their limbs one way, as if craving alms of the sun.

(chapter 1)

Lockwood's description of the exterior of the house is stark:

The narrow windows are deeply set in the wall, and the corners defended with large jutting stones.

(chapter 1)

and for much of the novel barred gates and locked doors confirm the inhospitable ways of the house. It repels visitors — Lockwood at the beginning and even Nelly later on (her final epithet for it is 'grim'). Conversely it acts as a prison — as children, Catherine and Heathcliff are glad to break out from it 'one awful Sunday' (chapter 3, chapter 6) and Lockwood, Isabella, Linton, young Catherine and Nelly are all at some stage forcibly detained inside it. But although Wuthering Heights is so often unwelcoming, guarded by fierce dogs and fiercer inmates, it is sometimes seen more positively. It is essentially a farm; there are working horses, sheep in folds and haymaking in the fields, in which the whole household is involved. Despite the promise of the house's future, empty and barricaded, our final experience of it is quite the opposite. As Lockwood approaches for the last time:

I had neither to climb the gate nor to knock — it yielded to my hand.

(chapter 32)

And instead of neglect and waste there is a garden and growth:

... a fragrance of stocks and wallflowers wafted on the air, from among the homely fruit trees.

(chapter 32)

It is a brief vision of paradise restored — Wuthering Heights transformed from the hell that it had represented to so many of the characters in the novel.

From within, the house has a marvellous solidity. Although there is a clear social distinction between the 'house' (the main living room) and the kitchen, these rooms share at their worst a primitive lack of comfort and at their best a homely atmosphere centred on a glowing hearth. Nelly describes an interior tableau which captures the last moment of fireside happiness before the death of old Mr Earnshaw ushers in the years of unhappiness at Wuthering Heights:

> ... we were all together — I a little removed from the hearth, busy at my knitting, and Joseph reading his Bible near the table (for the servants generally sat in the house then, after their work was done). Miss Cathy had been sick, and that made her still; she leant against her father's knee, and Heathcliff was lying on the floor with his head in her lap.
>
> (chapter 5)

Such physical and social harmony is contrasted absolutely with the empty elegance of the drawing-room at Thrushcross Grange:

> ... a splendid place carpeted in crimson, and crimson-covered chairs and tables, and a pure white ceiling bordered by gold, a shower of glass drops hanging in silver chains from the centre, and shimmering with little soft tapers.
>
> (chapter 6)

In the Wuthering Heights scene, old Mr Earnshaw is stroking Cathy's hair as she sings him to sleep. In the Thrushcross Grange scene the parents are out and the Linton children are at opposite ends of the room, having quarrelled over a lap-dog. Significantly Thrushcross Grange is first described by Heathcliff; he is the narrator for this scene and it is the one time he shows any awareness of place and atmosphere. He is excluded from the privileged life it encapsulates and, although he spends years scheming to acquire the Grange, it is done out of envy and revenge, to spite the Lintons; he could never live there. For Catherine, however, the glimpse into pampered luxury is the start of a different sort of corruption which will lead her to choose marriage to Edgar Linton in preference to the 'degradation' of Heathcliff. At Thrushcross Grange she will live in a parlour, exiled from her true home. Thereafter a key theme of her unhappiness will be her longing to return to Wuthering Heights.

'Home' (as estate agents well know) is not just a synonym for 'house' but expresses an attitude, a feeling of security and being. Although the passionate attitudes are those of Hindley, Catherine and Heathcliff, it is the strong, steady presence of Nelly Dean which actually creates a home out of a house. She 'keeps house', nurses, nourishes. The hearth is her domain. She can be superstitious, officious, deceitful, insensitive, but she embodies the sane, healthy values of ordinary human beings. It is to Nelly, rocking a baby on her lap in the kitchen, that Catherine comes to confide her own doubts and ask for advice. When Nelly leaves, Wuthering Heights degenerates. Isabella describes the 'inhospitable hearth', the 'dingy, untidy hole' of a kitchen and how the floor, once Nelly's pride and delight, 'had grown a uniform grey; and the once brilliant pewter dishes . . . partook of a similar obscurity, created by tarnish and dust' (chapter 13). Although by the time Lockwood enters the house it is once again warm and clean, thanks to Zillah, the atmosphere is anything but homely and it is not until Nelly returns that life starts to flourish again. At first a formal parlour is established, in imitation of Thrushcross Grange and to keep young Catherine out of Heathcliff's way. But the friendship and love between her and Hareton is specifically fostered by Nelly in an informal setting, 'while I ironed or pursued other stationary employment I could not well do in the parlour' (chapter 32).

However, the sense of home that is focused on the hearth is domestic, a comfortable but perhaps limited vision. Catherine's first vision, the dream she describes to Nelly, is more disturbing and profound:

> . . . heaven did not seem to be my home; and I broke my heart with weeping to come back to earth; and the angels were so angry that they flung me out into the middle of the heath on the top of Wuthering Heights; where I woke sobbing for joy.
>
> (chapter 9)

One realises here that the Wuthering Heights which moves Catherine to such joy is not so much the house as the heath; it is the landscape as much as the building that embodies her heaven. In locality, as in architecture and furnishing, Wuthering Heights is contrasted with Thrushcross Grange. Though linked by the sound of the beck, the two places are utterly distinct. The moorland is wild and unconfined, whereas the parkland is ordered and enclosed; the one offers danger and

Beatrice believes unequivocably that she will go to heaven. "Get me to heaven" Beatrice

the heath not the building

→ heath and building seem to Catherine to be mutually inclusive

excitement whereas the other offers security and peace. The high heath is the element of Heathcliff (think of his name); the park down the valley shelters the civilised Edgar Linton. In choosing the latter, Catherine is doomed to painful yearning for the former, the true home of her spirit:

> I'm sure I should be myself were I once among the heather on those hills.

> → As does Shakespeare

(chapter 12)

Brontë uses landscape metaphorically — its features and changing aspects can express states of mind or spirit. In the second generation the original polarisation of character is modified as the genes mix, and the result is evident in the cousins' imaginations. Young Linton's idea of happiness is:

> . . . lying from morning till evening on a bank of heath in the middle of the moors, with the bees humming dreamily about among the bloom, and the larks singing high up overhead, and the blue sky and bright sun shining steadily and cloudlessly.

(chapter 24)

Young Catherine's is:

> . . . rocking in a rustling green tree, with a west wind blowing, and bright white clouds flitting rapidly above; and not only larks but throstles, and blackbirds, and linnets, and cuckoos pouring out music on every side, and the moors seen at a distance, broken into cool dusky dells . . .

(chapter 24)

Interestingly both these scenes really derive from Nelly's own harmonising (perhaps compromising) view. When the reluctant Linton was dispatched to his new and alien 'home' it was Nelly who sowed the germ of his future pleasure:

> It is not so buried in trees . . . you can see the country beautifully all around; and the air is healthier . . . fresher, dryer . . . And you will have such nice rambles on the moors.

(chapter 20)

And it is Nelly who has delighted in the lively spark which drives young Catherine, instead of walking demurely beneath the garden trees, to 'sit in the branches, swinging twenty feet above the ground' (chapter 22). Although the polarised view of Wuthering Heights and Thrushcross Grange is crucial to the plot of the novel and helps to express the theme of Catherine's betrayal, Nelly's more accommodating view is important. She can see happiness in both localities. In fact the landscape of the moors is, in *Wuthering Heights*, much more sweet than harsh. It is bleak and repellent at first, answering Lockwood's preconceived romantic notions of what is proper to the rural desolation of a 'misanthropist's heaven' (chapter 1). But more often the moors are balmy, blooming and full of birdsong:

> The sky is blue and the larks are singing, and the becks and brooks are all brim full ... I wish you were a mile or two up those hills: the air blows so sweetly ...
>
> (chapter 13)

This lyrical description is by Edgar Linton. Edgar, of course, comes to love the moors because he loves Catherine. Lockwood's vision also develops. This is his final description as he looks at the three graves on the edge of the moor:

> I lingered round them, under that benign sky: watched the moths fluttering among the heath and harebells; listened to the soft wind breathing through the grass.
>
> (chapter 34)

The graves are the end of a story that really begins in a bed — the panelled bed in which Lockwood has his terrible encounter with the spirit of Catherine. Both bed and grave are fashioned for resting; they are uncannily parallel places. At the height of her second fever (chapter 12), Catherine is haunted by an image: 'I thought I was at home ... I thought I was lying in my bed at Wuthering Heights,' and again: 'Oh, if I were but in my own bed in the old house! ... And the wind sounding in the firs by the lattice'. To the reader, perhaps sharing Lockwood's original experience in the chamber, it seems eery and disturbing; and in fact Catherine's own associations are not really of comfort. She relates her delirious conviction 'that I was enclosed in the oak-panelled bed at home; and my heart ached with some great grief which, just waking, I could not recollect'. Then she identifies the grief of seven years previously: 'My misery arose from the separation that Hindley had ordered between me and Heathcliff. I was laid alone for the first time.' The memory plunges her into 'a paroxysm of despair'. The bed had originally represented the united security of Catherine's childhood (just as scampering over the moors represented its happy freedom). The moment of physical separation forced by Hindley is relived as Catherine recognises the spiritual separation which she herself imposed in choosing Edgar and denying Heathcliff, her 'soul'. Her spirit haunts Wuthering Heights, struggling to re-enter the bed-chamber through the locked window; but it cannot. When Heathcliff flings open the window and calls to her, there is no reply, only 'the snow and the wind whirled wildly' (chapter 3). The spiritual reunion is denied until, twenty-five years after the first separation, Heathcliff lies dead at that same bedroom window. His hand resting across the sill, grazed by the flapping of the open lattice, strikingly recalls Lockwood's image of Catherine's wrist rubbed across the broken pane of the lattice until 'the blood ran down'.

The grave is a second, and permanent, bed. Catherine pictures it with yearning:

> . . . my narrow home out yonder; my resting place, where I'm bound before spiring is over! There it is; not among the Lintons, mind, under the chapel-roof, but in the open air, with a head-stone . . .
>
> (chapter 19)

She is indeed buried as she wishes. Nelly describes the place:

> . . . on a green slope in a corner of the kirkyard, where the wall is so low that heath and bilberry plants have climbed over it from the moor . . .
>
> (chapter 16)

To Edgar it is the place where he seems to achieve a peaceful union with his wife. Catherine had (in chapter 12) imagined her body at rest in the grave while her spirit, freed from the 'shattered prison' of her body, would escape into the 'glorious world' of a disembodied life with Heathcliff. Heathcliff is less hopeful of spiritual ecstacy; he wants physical union, and secures it in the mingling of his decomposed body with Catherine's in the moorland soil. For both, death is the liberating agent.

But time is stronger than death. Time will allow Edgar's

body also to mingle with Catherine's and that of his rival — all three 'rolled round in earth's diurnal course,/ With rocks, and stones, and trees' (Wordsworth, 'A slumber did my spirit seal'). The two chief narrators seem to share the comforting philosophy which those lines imply. Nelly, having buried Catherine with a locket in which the light and dark hairs of her two opposed lovers are harmoniously intertwined, says, 'I believe the dead are at peace' and concentrates on the living harmony of their descendants. Lockwood, after a snigger about 'ghosts', is happy to concur and ends the novel wondering:

> . . . how anyone could ever imagine unquiet slumbers for the sleepers in that quiet earth.

> (chapter 34)

Of course *we* can, because Brontë's vision is not so simply comforting as that of her narrators. It is difficult to finish the novel without believing in the reality of the spiritual dimension within it. The 'happy-ever-after' urge makes us wish that young Catherine and Hareton would live on in the summer-time Wuthering Heights with its new and flourishing garden, asserting the reassuring doctrine of joy out of sadness, life out of death. But such a resolution would be false to Wuthering Heights — the house, the place and what it represents. Wuthering Heights is, finally, an atmosphere, a frame of mind — stormy and turbulent (wuthering), exalted and isolated (heights). The original Catherine and Heathcliff belong in that invigorating element, but they are eternal outcasts from the humdrum world of more ordinary mortals. Wuthering Heights, the place that embodies their suffering and their bliss, must be left to them.

AFTERTHOUGHTS

1

What image of *Wuthering Heights* did *you* have before you read the novel?

2

In what ways does Brontë use landscape 'metaphorically' (page 25)?

3

What parallels does Saunders draw in this essay between graves and beds?

4

Compare Saunders's interpretation of the novel's last sentence (page 28) with Cheetham's view of it in the next essay (page 38).

Paul Cheetham

Paul Cheetham has extensive experience as a teacher of English Literature and as a GCE examiner. He is currently a Research Fellow in the Department of Education at Edinburgh University.

ESSAY

Wuthering Heights as a ghost-story

Approximately eighty years before Emily Brontë sat down to write *Wuthering Heights*, Horace Walpole published a novel called *The Castle of Otranto*, which represented a reaction against the order, elegance and rationalism of the Age of Enlightenment which had dawned and blossomed in the eighteenth century. As he himself put it in his Preface to the second edition of his novel (1765), when referring to his fellow-authors of the period:

> Invention has not been wanting; but the great resources of fancy have been dammed up by a strict adherence to common life.

Walpole's own formula for entertaining and unnerving the readers of *The Castle of Otranto* was disarmingly simple: skeletons deliver sermons, a portrait comes to life, a statue bleeds, and supernatural forces take a direct hand in exposing and thwarting usurpers by killing one with a giant helmet and flattening the walls of a castle to dispose of another. Whereas the sophisticated modern reader may find such crudities merely ludicrous, Walpole's contemporaries had no difficulty in explaining the appeal of such literature:

The more wild, fanciful and extraordinary are the circumstances of a scene of horror, the more pleasure we receive from it.

(J and L Aiken, *On the pleasure derived from objects of terror*, 1775)

and while our literary tastes may have changed, there is no doubt that the huge popularity of horror films bears out the truth of such a comment.

Walpole's book spawned a whole succession of similar, so-called 'Gothic' novels by authors such as Clara Reeve, William Beckford and 'Monk' Lewis, and it was some fifty years before this literary vein was fully worked out. However, in the early part of the nineteenth century, largely as a result of the growing influence of Coleridge's poetry and literary criticism, the tide begun to turn in the direction of a more intense and concentrated exploration of strange phenomena. Writers increasingly concerned themselves with profound questions: the relationship between dreams and everyday life; the exploration and definition of abnormal mental conditions. The result of these reflections was an important change in technique. Events were no longer, for the most part, put forward as an objective reality, related by an omniscient narrator, but as an experience. Authors tended increasingly to present their narratives in the words of those who had experienced them, and left the readers to form their own interpretations and draw their own conclusions. These authors were working towards that perfect balance between subjective impression and objective fact, which, without challenging the reader to a total acceptance or rejection, leaves the nagging feeling that something has happened which is strange, unaccountable and, in purely human terms, ultimately inexplicable. Such was the literary tradition out of which *Wuthering Heights* emerged.

The narrative technique devised by Emily Brontë for *Wuthering Heights* plays a crucial part in the novel's effectiveness, and from the outset we form a marked impression of the main narrator, Lockwood. Although he brings with him a degree of southern smoothness and sophistication, which is repeatedly contrasted with the northern roughness and ruggedness which he finds 'up there' (indicating, incidentally, that he sees himself as addressing a southern readership), within a few pages of the novel's opening we learn that his awkwardness and shyness have only recently (and not for the first or last time, we may surmise) prevented him from forming a close relationship with a member of the opposite sex. He has, in fact, retired to this 'perfect misanthropist's heaven' (chapter 1) in the North of England expressly in order to lick his emotional wounds. His reserve and lack of ease in company are reflected in his diction, which is strained, pompous and highly formal. His opening words to Heathcliff exemplify this:

> ... I do myself the honour of calling as soon as possible after my arrival, to express the hope that I have not inconvenienced you by my perseverance in soliciting the occupation of Thrush-cross Grange ...
>
> (chapter 1)

No wonder Heathcliff interrupts him? He is strangely, almost naïvely literal-minded and in swift succession commits a series of blunders and misjudgements, some of which are merely embarrassing, while others cause him varying degrees of physical discomfort, ranging from being initially denied tea to twice being set about by Heathcliff's dogs.

The opening two chapters, then, are important for building up in our minds the picture of an observer who is a complete outsider, who, for all his enthusiastically claimed emotional kinship with Heathcliff, has little comprehension of the strange world in which he now finds himself, whose vision is limited and prosaic and whose judgement is at best questionable. The third chapter of *Wuthering Heights* is remarkable for the way in which it moves the action from the starkly, almost aggressively physical plane, which characterises the first two chapters, onto a different level altogether, on which it intermittently operates for the rest of the novel. The change begins once Lockwood is shut inside the box-bed: we are confronted by a host of Catherines — Earnshaw, Linton, Heathcliff — evidently the romantic fantasies of a young girl; we are given an apparently artless reference to 'a date some quarter of a century back'; we are also presented with a grim, penitential picture of conventional religion, coupled with references to Catherine's and Heathcliff's spirited rejection of it; and we are incidentally given an illuminating insight into Catherine's and Heathcliff's attitude towards conventional expressions of heterosexual love in her contemptuous description of Hindley and Frances, 'like two babies, kissing and talking nonsense by the hour — foolish palaver that we should be ashamed of'.

Under the influence of these varied stimuli, it is scarcely surprising that even the unimaginative and unimpressionable Lockwood should begin to dream, but what is interesting is the difference between the two dreams that Emily Brontë inflicts on him. The first is wholly derived from a combination of his disagreeable experiences at Wuthering Heights and the words that he has been reading. These are fancifully developed and elaborated into the kind of nightmare with which most of us are familiar, but there is nothing about the dream to make us think that anything other than Lockwood's subconscious mind is at work, reshaping his experience into a grimly humorous parody of Joseph's religious attitude and observance. The only external element incorporated in the dream is the naturalistic tapping of the branch on the lattice, which briefly restores Lockwood to consciousness and acts as a bridge to his next, and very different, dream. In this one the elements become much more complicated and confused, as do, in consequence, the boundaries between this world and the next. The first intermingling of the real world and the other, metaphysical, world comes in the reference to the window hasp, when Lockwood discovers that 'the hook was soldered into the staple: a circumstance observed by me when awake, but forgotten'. Immediately after that, Lockwood himself expresses surprise when the voice which accompanies the ice-cold hand refers to its owner as Catherine Linton: 'Why did I think of *Linton?* I had read *Earnshaw* twenty times for Linton.' And finally there is the apparently casual reference to the time-scale: '"Begone!" I shouted; "I'll never let you in, not if you beg for twenty years." "It is twenty years," mourned the voice, "twenty years. I've been a waif for twenty years!"'

Now there is clearly a risk of being too literal-minded in our interpretation of such statements, but in view of the very careful dating-scheme which Emily Brontë used in this book (see C P Sanger's essay on 'The Structure of Wuthering Heights', in I Gregor (ed.), *Twentieth Century Views: The Brontës* — Englewood Cliffs, NJ, 1970), it may be worth pausing for a moment to look at what happened at Wuthering Heights in or about 1781, twenty years before Lockwood's dream. From the beginning of chapter 4 it appears that Catherine married Edgar Linton in 1783, and in chapter 9 the references to dates make it clear that the marriage took place three years after the deaths of Edgar's parents and Heathcliff's nocturnal disappearance from Wuthering Heights. It would, of course, be absurd to expect both Lockwood and his dream-interlocutor to be absolutely precise about dates; besides, the figure twenty is already running in his head, as we have seen above. However, it is at least tempting to speculate that when the ghostly Catherine replies, 'I've been a waif for twenty years,' she may be referring to her separation from Heathcliff rather than to her marriage to Edgar.

The final point to make about the second dream is that its implications receive confirmation from Heathcliff when he flings open the window: '"Come in! come in!" he sobbed. "Cathy, do come. Oh do — once more! Oh! my heart's darling! hear me this time, Catherine, at last!"', on which Lockwood comments with unconscious and, doubtless, unintentionally heartless irony, 'The spectre showed a spectre's ordinary caprice: it gave no sign of being'.

Lockwood's second dream, then, is a classic example of the ghost-story writer's technique in operation. The whole experience exists in that strange world in which fact and fancy mingle. Most of what happens in the dream can be explained away by reference to the stimuli to which Lockwood has been subjected, yet there is a residual element which lies beyond those and which depends upon prior knowledge, which, at this stage in the book, is not yet in Lockwood's possession. At the same time — and most convincingly of all — Lockwood himself appears curiously unaffected by the experience. His compassion for Heathcliff and to some extent his curiosity are aroused, but when, at the beginning of chapter 4, he begins to question Nelly Dean, he does so out of a desire for company rather than from any wish to get to the bottom of his dream. On this occasion, as elsewhere in the book, Lockwood's prosaic, matter-of-fact nature remains intact.

For all Lockwood's own indifference to the implications of his narrative, its supernatural suggestiveness is reinforced in

their relationship does not transcend religion

suggests that her Christian principle(s) will allow her to feel better psychologically, as much as her relationship with B

various ways in succeeding chapters. First there
references to Heathcliff's nature and origins. M
himself unwittingly launches these by light-hearte
Heathcliff as being 'as dark almost as if it came fı
(chapter 4) and his satanic disposition is thereafter a recurring
motif throughout the book. 'He bred bad feeling in the house,'
Nelly recalls (chaper 4); Hindley abuses him as an 'imp of Satan'
(ibid.); Nelly semi-seriously refers to his eyes as 'black fiends
... like devil's spies' (chapter 7) and later remarks, 'it
appeared as if the lad were possessed of something diabolical at
that period' (chapter 8). Once married to him, Isabella speculates in terror, 'Is Mr Heathcliff a man? If so, is he mad? And
if not, is he a devil?' (chapter 13), and after she has run away
from him she expresses her views with more certainty: 'He's not
a human being ... Whether the angels have fed him, or his kin
beneath, I cannot tell' (chapter 17). These scattered diabolical
hints are amplified by references to the obscurity of his origins,
his unexplained three-year disappearance in the middle of the
novel and the mystery of the source of his new-found wealth on
his return (see Nelly's reflections in chapter 10).

If, however, this all strikes the modern reader as an un-
necessarily heavy-handed reiteration, it contributes to a more
important element in the novel, the rejection of conventional
religion. The rebellious daughter of the rector of Howarth
created two protagonists utterly hostile to traditional Christian
concepts of heaven as the ultimate goal. The most forceful and
outspoken articulation of this rejection comes in that crucial
chapter, chapter 9, when Catherine tells Nelly how she once
dreamed that she was in heaven, 'and heaven did not seem to
be my home; and I broke my heart with weeping to come back
to earth; and the angels were so angry that they flung me out
into the middle of the heath on top of Wuthering Heights; where
I woke sobbing for joy'.

Yet although Catherine's view of eternal bliss is wholly
unconventional, she has an utter conviction about a spiritual
existence beyond the physical: 'I cannot express it', she tells
Nelly, 'but surely you and everybody have a notion that there
is or should be an existence of yours beyond you. What were the
use of creation if I were entirely contained here?' (chapter 9).
Hand in hand with this goes her belief in spiritual union, indeed

so whilst not Christian, she is
spiritual.
contrasts with MEANS:
"serve God, love me, and mend"

because this means
rules!

identification, with Heathcliff: 'He's more myself than I am,' she tells Nelly. 'If all else perished and he remained, I should still continue to be . . . I *am* Heathcliff! He's always, always in my mind; not as a pleasure, any more than I am always a pleasure to myself, but as my own being. So don't talk of our separation again.' (chapter 9).

Of course, in marrying Edgar Linton, Catherine denies her own nature and inflicts years of suffering on both herself and Heathcliff (not to mention Edgar and, indirectly, Isabella and Hareton). Yet at the same time the very idea of marriage between Heathcliff and Catherine seems quite absurdly irrelevant and inappropriate. From an early stage in the book the reader has a sense of their frustration with the limitations of ordinary earthly existence. The violence and agony of their embraces at their meetings in the days leading up to Catherine's death (chapter 15) suggest a desperate yearning to transcend these limitations and enjoy a true and total metaphysical union. As Catherine says, 'I'm tired, tired of being enclosed here. I'm wearying to escape into that glorious world and to be always there.' (ibid.).

Yet Catherine's release from the world brings relief to neither herself nor Heathcliff. As we have seen, chapter 3 strongly suggests that the restless ghost of Catherine is still seeking reunion with her lost love, and her death leaves Heathcliff in an intolerable vacuum: 'Where is she? Not *there* — not in heaven — not perished — where? . . . Be with me always — take any form — drive me mad! only *do* not leave me in this abyss where I cannot find you! Oh, God! it is unutterable! I *cannot* live without my life! I *cannot* live without my soul!' (chapter 16).

In the frustration brought about by his separation from Catherine, Heathcliff's diabolical nature asserts itself in a single-minded programme of vengeful appropriation and degradation, sustained and intensified, as he explains to Nelly, by the constant sense of Catherine's being just out of his reach (chapter 29). The desire for total revenge begins to abate only when Heathcliff's frustration, which has lasted almost twenty years, gives way at last to an eager anticipation of ultimate and eternal reunion.

The final chapter of the novel charts Heathcliff's developing detachment from life, as the reader gradually becomes aware that Heathcliff is, in some sense, in communication — or perhaps communion would be a more appropriate word — with Catherine. The first clear hint of this comes with the reference at the beginning of chapter 34 to his nocturnal rambles, and the evidence hardens with the description of his curious behaviour at meals. At first whatever it is that engages Heathcliff's attention is relatively remote: 'He took his knife and fork and was going to commence eating, when the inclination appeared to become suddenly extinct. He laid them on the table, looked eagerly towards the window, then rose and went out'. (chapter 34). (At this point it is worth remarking that windows, which have an important symbolic function throughout the novel, become an increasingly prominent feature in the last chapter.) When Nelly questions Heathcliff about his behaviour, he gives a partial explanation: 'Last night I was on the threshold of hell. Today, I am within sight of heaven.' (ibid.).

On the second occasion when Nelly concerns herself with feeding him, his abstraction is even more pronounced: 'With a sweep of his hand he cleared a vacant space in front among the breakfast things, and leant forward to gaze more at his ease' (ibid.), and the suggestion that he is absorbed in the contemplation of some kind of vision is unmistakable: 'Now, I perceived he was not looking at the wall; for when I regarded him alone, it seemed exactly that he gazed at something within two yards' distance.' (ibid.).

The place and manner of Heathcliff's death turn the wheel full circle to Lockwood's dream in chapter 3. The setting is once again the box-bed; the window is the threshold between the two worlds; there is even the graze on Heathcliff's hand to join him with the spirit whose wrist Lockwood had so cruelly rubbed to and fro on the broken window-pane. The clear implication of this accumulation of detail is that Heathcliff and Catherine have at last been mystically reunited.

For all Nelly's professed scepticism about the rumours of Heathcliff's ghost haunting the moor and the house, powerful confirmation is afforded by the account of the terrified shepherd boy's refusal to pass the spot where he has seen 'Heathcliff and a woman . . . under t'nab'. He himself is, of course, too young ever to have known Catherine, and in case the reader is still doubtful about his reliability as a witness, Emily Brontë enlists the behaviour of his flock in his support.

Lockwood, however, in spite of all the assaults on his imagination repeated at intervals throughout the novel, retains his pedestrian cast of mind to the last. In doing so he is surely intended by the author to provoke in the reader a very different reaction from that which he intends to convey by his closing words, of whose ambiguity he seems so blithely unaware: 'I lingered round them, under that benign sky; watched the moths fluttering among the heath and harebells, listened to the soft wind breathing through the grass, and wondered how anyone could ever imagine unquiet slumbers for the sleepers in that quiet earth' (chapter 34). Paradoxically, Lockwood's earthbound incomprehension is the medium which Emily Brontë shrewdly chose to break down the reader's natural resistance to a story which so deliberately blurs the distinctions between this world and the next.

AFTERTHOUGHTS

1

What significance does Cheetham attach to the ghost's claim to have 'been a waif for *twenty* years' (page 33)?

2

Do you agree that the novel rejects 'conventional religion' (page 35)?

3

Compare Cheetham's view of the last sentence of the novel (page 38) with Saunders's interpretation in the previous essay (page 28).

4

Does *Wuthering Heights* suggest to you that Brontë believed literally in the existence of ghosts?

Cedric Watts

Cedric Watts is Professor of English at Sussex University, and author of numerous scholarly publications.

ESSAY

Tensions in the characterisation of Heathcliff

1

Wuthering Heights is a rich, dense, bold, artfully structured and thematically complex novel which offers a very thorough exploration of the attractions, perils and tensions of romanticism. The romantic movement burgeoned in the late eighteenth and early nineteenth centuries, and, for better and for worse, its influence still continues. What made it attractive was its advocacy of intense, passionate selfhood. What made it perilous was its advocacy of egoistic, anarchic and destructive conduct. One of the tensions in romanticism is this: sometimes the writings commend sociability (perhaps the sociability of a warm, loving family unit), and sometimes they commend the antisocial — the hero may be a lonely egoist who, in the pursuit of self-fulfilment, is prepared to disrupt the lives of others. In 1946 the philosopher Bertrand Russell, writing at the end of a war provoked by the fascism which he saw as partly a consequence of romanticism, stated:

The romantic movement, in its essence, aimed at liberating human personality from the fetters of social convention and social morality. In part, these fetters were a mere useless hindrance to more desirable forms of activity ... But egoistic passions, when once let loose, are not easily brought again into subjection to the needs of society ... Egoism, at first, made men expect from others a parental tenderness; but when they discovered, with indignation, that others had their own Ego, the disappointed desire for tenderness turned to hatred and violence. Man is not a solitary animal, and so long as social life survives, self-realisation cannot be the supreme principle of ethics.

(Bertrand Russell, *A History of Western Philosophy* Bk 3, Pt 2, ch. XVII — London, 1946)

Much of Russell's attack on romanticism has been vigorously anticipated by *Wuthering Heights*, in its depiction of Heathcliff's cruelties and tyrannies and in its demonstration that the developing love and cooperation of Hareton and the second Cathy make his triumph hollow and futile. The text, however, also makes the case for 'Heathcliff as hero' — as a person whose very intensity of being imposes itself on the imagination and makes the more conventional people of his world seem less vital. The novel thus displays a battle between traditional moral criteria (which commend constructive, law-abiding conduct) and the claim that sheer vitality of being is superior to conventionality of being.

2

When I discuss *Wuthering Heights* with undergraduates, I often find that different students seem to be seeing different Heathcliffs; it's a sign of the novel's complexity. So in this section I'm going to survey rapidly the different aspects of Heathcliff that such discussions have brought to light.

Some students see Heathcliff predominantly as an enigma, and they point out that the Catherine who so memorably and quotably epitomises her love for Heathcliff in the words 'Nelly, I *am* Heathcliff' (chapter 9) is the same Catherine who (in chapter 19) warns Isabella about him:

Pray, don't imagine that he conceals depths of benevolence and affection beneath a stern exterior! He's not a rough diamond — a pearl-containing oyster of a rustic; he's a fierce, pitiless, wolfish man.

Nevertheless, Isabella finds him so desirable that she gladly elopes with him and estranges herself from her brother and home; yet within two months of her marriage she writes to Nelly Dean:

Is Mr Heathcliff a man? If so, is he mad? And if not, is he a devil? . . . I beseech you to explain, if you can, what I have married . . .

(chapter 13)

Emphatically, then, *Wuthering Heights* establishes Heathcliff's character as an enigma, deeply layered, strange and baffling to others. It is one of the ways (others being the doubly oblique narrative method and the apparent subordination of conventional plotting to thematic patterning) by which this novel of 1847 anticipates some features of modernist texts of the period 1890–1930; which is further evidence of the pervasive influence of romanticism. A central aspect of the 'enigma' of Heathcliff is the obvious paradox that he, though conspicuously 'pitiless' and 'wolfish', is charismatically attractive — briefly so to Isabella, permanently so to Catherine. A perennial, familiar point, a point sharpened vigorously in the romantic period, is that passionate sexual love may subvert moral judgement; and this relates to the novel's wider discussion of the power of sheer vital intensity to subvert ethical orthodoxy. Interpretations of Heathcliff which seek to offer a clear summary of his nature may ignore the fact that one of the main suspense-principles of the narrative has been the maintenance of the enigmatic element; there is an opacity in him, a volatility and a range of possibilities, which to the end keeps us in some doubt about what he will do. Brontë's nurturing of the enigma may question not only the tendency of conventional novels to present characters as clearly knowable, but also our tendency in life to assume that the natures of others retain a rational consistency.

There are several holes or lacunae in the story of Heathcliff. First, we know nothing for certain about his origins. Mr Earnshaw brings home a starving houseless infant whom he has found in the streets of Liverpool. This ignorance of Heathcliff's parentage and background helps to generate and sustain the enigma of his nature. Earnshaw says, '. . . you must e'en take it as a gift of God; though it's as dark almost as if it came from the devil'. (Gift of God? Son of the devil? Illegitimate offspring of a Liverpudlian sailor? Abandoned child of gipsies?) Nelly remarks of his history, 'It's a cuckoo's' (chapter 4); and Heathcliff, an outsider who eventually engrosses the estate into which he intrudes, does resemble the cuckoo which, reared in another bird's nest, pushes aside the weaker fledglings to advance itself. And, of course, one of the main ironies of the plot is that Nelly, attempting to cheer the young Heathcliff by offering a fancifully exalted notion of his origins, seems herself to have suggested to him the idea of the economic revenge that he eventually takes against the Earnshaw and Linton families:

> Who knows, but your father was Emperor of China, and your mother an Indian queen, each of them able to buy up, with one week's income, Wuthering Heights and Thrushcross Grange together?

> (chapter 7)

If he's a cuckoo in the nest, becoming owner of the home that was not originally his own, Nelly may unwittingly have given him that ambition. The second gap in the characterisation of Heathcliff occurs when, believing himself to be scorned by Cathy, he runs away. Three years later he reappears transformed: now commanding, confident and outwardly gentlemanly, possessed of money which he increases by gambling at cards with Hindley. What he did during those crucial three years is never explained. Again, the text offers speculations (perhaps he had served in the army) but no certainties.

The third gap concerns his courtship of Isabella, of which we are given a few glimpses and hints but no full account. In this case, the authorial reticence may veil the improbability that Heathcliff could conceal his contempt for Isabella sufficiently to sustain the lover's role. A fuller presentation might make Isabella's infatuation seem incredibly short-sighted.

The fourth gap concerns the sexuality of his relationship with Cathy before her marriage. The intensity of their bond may give the reader the impression that they have had a fully sexual relationship, but the text provides no confirmation; here (not unexpectedly in a nineteenth-century novel) the narrative veils what a more recent novel would have treated explicitly. Bertrand Russell has suggested that romantic egotism accounts for the interest in incestuous or semi-incestuous sexuality which becomes prominent during the romantic period (the egoistic lover seeking a partner who is an extension or reflection of himself or herself);[1] and though Heathcliff and Cathy are not blood-relatives, they have the closeness of siblings in their early life together.

However, while some students emphasise the enigmas in Heathcliff's story, other students go further and suggest that he belongs to a historic 'family' of literary characters: characters which may have been influenced by Edmund Burke's theories and which become prominent in the 'Gothic' novels — the popular fiction of the late eighteenth and early nineteenth centuries.

Edmund Burke's very influential treatise, *A Philosophical Enquiry into the Origin of Our Ideas of the Sublime and Beautiful* (1757), had said that whereas our sense of beauty is related to our sexual and sociable feelings, our sense of the sublime is related to the feelings of pain and fear. In particular, objects arousing a sense of the sublime offer, or evoke memories of, a threat to our self-preservation: such objects may be powerful, rugged, dark, obscure and mysterious. This theory influenced not only the favoured locations in Gothic novels (craggy mountainous regions, gloomy forests, ominous ruins, subterranean vaults), but also the characterisation of the Gothic 'hero-villains' — and Heathcliff is, among other things, a member of that large literary family. In Gothic narratives, a central figure is commonly the charismatic villain: he is mysterious, saturnine, brooding, powerful, ruthless, sexually menacing, tyrannical, a night-creature gripped by dark or evil ambitions. Sometimes he is accursed and haunted (like Manfred in Walpole's *Castle of Otranto* or Montoni in Radcliffe's *Mysteries of Udolpho*); sometimes he has literally made a pact with the

---

[1] Op. cit.

devil, like Ambrosio in Lewis's *The Monk*. Such characters are distantly overshadowed by Milton's Satan, that figure of obdurate yet courageous ambition, and more distantly by Marlowe's Dr Faustus, who was prepared to sell his soul in order to gain earthly power. When Heathcliff returns after his mysterious absence, he seems possessed of new potency and destructiveness, other characters increasingly refer to him as evil, hellish or diabolical, and he proves to be invincibly successful in his economic conquests. Eventually, however, his victory loses its savour, he relinquishes his grip on his surviving victims, and perishes.

A supernatural dimension (a common feature of Gothic novels) is certainly invoked, intermittently, by the narrative, even though *Wuthering Heights* generally provides a secular, natural explanation of seemingly supernatural events. Heathcliff's sense of an afterlife is distinctive and unorthodox: not for him a conventional heaven or hell, but a union — he imagines — with Cathy in the earth and on the heath, roaming this world after death. He belongs to the romantic élite of intense, driven characters whose contempt for mundane values can be seen now as a noble exaltation and now as an ultimately suicidal dementia.

I find that left-wing students, however, are often less interested in the supernatural elements of the narrative than in the 'Godwinian' theme. William Godwin's *Enquiry Concerning Political Justice* (1793), a key-text of romanticism, had argued that men are basically good but are corrupted by oppressive institutions; people who are treated tyrannically may become tyrants in their turn; and private property is a potent corrupting force. Frankenstein's monster (in Mary Shelley's novel *Frankenstein*) proves to be a true Godwinian when he declares 'I was benevolent and good; misery made me a fiend'. Heathcliff's career recalls, in part, the Godwinian thesis; for he is initially treated harshly by Catherine, Hindley and even Nelly; as he grows up, he is vindictively thrust into the role of servant by Hindley; he believes that Cathy prefers Edgar Linton because Edgar has wealth and social graces; and, embittered, he returns to inflict on others the injustices he believes he had once received, and to appropriate for himself the weapon of wealth.

Of course, this kind of summary may make the plot of

Wuthering Heights seem dangerously close to that of a melo-drama. Yet one remarkable feature of this novel is that though so many of its incidents seem, when considered in isolation or in summary, to be violently melodramatic, in context this material generally retains a surprising degree of plausibility. This is partly owing to the wealth of realistic detail in the depiction of the locality, the countryside, the domestic interiors, the work done, and the northern vernacular, and partly owing to the claustrophobic social scale, in which the anger, resent-ments and jealousies, close-confined, credibly breed and multiply. Plausibility does fade markedly, however, in two areas of the text: one is that presenting Heathcliff's harshness to Isabella, and the other is that depicting his cruelty to his grotesquely vile and puny son. At such points Heathcliff, in his malicious relish, comes demeaningly close to being the snarling, gloating and ogrish villain of nineteenth-century stage melo-drama. 'I have no pity! I have no pity! The more the worms writhe, the more I yearn to crush out their entrails!' (chapter 14): at these moments he sounds more like a Victorian ham-actor soliciting the hisses of his audience than the protagonist of a purportedly realistic novel. Emily Brontë's sister, Charlotte, may have been remembering those moments when she declared in 1850: 'Heathcliff, indeed, stands unredeemed; never once swerving in his arrow-straight course to perdition'.

I recall her view when I read students' essays which assure me that Heathcliff is not a wicked man but a force of nature, a 'child of storm'. Such essays are usually indebted to a chapter by Lord David Cecil in his book *Early Victorian Novelists* (London, 1934). Cecil says this about Heathcliff:

> He is not . . . as usually assumed, a wicked man voluntarily yielding to his wicked impulses. Like all Emily Brontë's charac-ters, he is a manifestation of natural forces acting involuntarily under the pressure of his own nature. But he is a natural force which has been frustrated of its natural outlet, so that it inevi-tably becomes destructive; like a mountain torrent diverted from its channel . . .

It is certainly the case that Heathcliff's obsession with Cathy is so titanic that it seems to deny him normal freedom of choice and action. Furthermore, the emotions of the characters are frequently described in terms of natural imagery, an imagery which seems highly appropriate to people living in that wild and windswept northern landscape. As Cathy remarks:

> My love for Linton is like the foliage in the woods. Time will change it, I'm well aware, as winter changes the trees. My love for Heathcliff resembles the eternal rocks beneath — a source of little visible delight, but necessary.
>
> (chapter 9)

The obvious objection to Lord David Cecil's view is that while one cannot offer a moral condemnation of 'a mountain torrent diverted from its channel', *Wuthering Heights* repeatedly offers and solicits moral judgements and condemnations of Heathcliff: he chooses to be deliberately destructive, and may be judged accordingly.

3

If we look back over this range of possibilities, we soon see why it is difficult to make a brief summary of Heathcliff's nature: his characterisation is layered, paradoxical and partly enigmatic. His long catalogue of crimes, bullying, brutality, malice, male chauvinism and emotional blackmail readily provokes condemnation. Nevertheless, against that, there are factors inviting moral lenience. He had an unfortunate early life (abandoned as an infant; later treated harshly by Hindley; then rejected for Edgar by Cathy); furthermore, with the exception of the well-nigh-incredible Linton Heathcliff, the people around him have plenty of energy to answer back and fight back — even Edgar has the power to silence him with a punch in the throat (chapter 11). It's also clear that for most of the time, even when he is materially successful, he seems to be suffering a hell or purgatory on earth: his monomania is its own punishment;[2] and some details of the text (notably Lockwood's vivid dream of Cathy)

---

[2] In marked contrast to Rochester in Charlotte Brontë's *Jane Eyre*, Heathcliff truculently declines to relapse into conventional pious penitence.

lend support to the notion that he is literally haunted by the dead. Another source of lenience is that, for better and for worse, romanticism continues to pervade our outlooks, so that we are inwardly impressed by the individual whose sheer obsessive intensity makes him seem more fully alive than relatively mundane people. But beware of sentimentalising Heathcliff as a superman among inferior beings. History offers many warnings against both sentimentality and supermen.

AFTERTHOUGHTS

1

What do you understand by 'romanticism' (opening paragraph)?

2

Why does Watts give such prominence to the ideas of Bertrand Russell at the beginning of this essay (page 41)?

3

Do you agree that *Wuthering Heights* repeatedly offers and solicits moral judgements and condemnations of Heathcliff (page 47)?

4

Why does this essay not identify a 'correct' view of Heathcliff's character?

Peter Hyland

*Peter Hyland is Senior Fellow of the
Centre for Reformation and Renaissance
Studies, Toronto. He is the author of
numerous scholarly publications.*

ESSAY

Wuthering Heights and the Gothic myth

Any reading of *Wuthering Heights* has to come to terms with the melodramatic or horror-comic aspects of the novel. What is the meaning of these tormented beings with their extravagant passions, these haunted, turbulent landscapes? How are we to take Heathcliff seriously, this near-superhuman protagonist who is frequently to be seen grinding or gnashing his teeth, or crushing his nails into his palms, or foaming like a mad dog, who hangs spaniels and tramples upon his enemy and is completely unconcerned about the death of his own son? Inevitably, much of the criticism of the novel has tended to consider it in terms of the emotional, psychological and spiritual state of its author, making it read as if it were the autobiography of a spiritually distressed personality, the lurid imaginings of a frustrated spinster condemned to a barren existence in an isolated Yorkshire village. However, while it is undeniable that the patterns of *Wuthering Heights* reflect Emily Brontë's own concerns, conscious or unconscious, it is also true that the novel's major symbols, its characters and landscapes, and the issues it embodies, have their roots in literature as much as in life. One source of the imaginative energy of *Wuthering Heights* is to be found in the tradition of the Gothic romance.

The Gothic romance is a form of fiction that flourished in the eighteenth and early nineteenth centuries, beginning with Horace Walpole's *The Castle of Otranto* (1764), and effectively ending with Charles Maturin's *Melmoth the Wanderer* (1820). Until quite recently the Gothic was a form despised by the majority of critics and dismissed as a vulgar and irrelevant fashion because of what they saw as its exploitation of cruelty and horror, its sensationalism, its stock mechanisms and melodramatic actions. A more sympathetic reading of these novels, however, has been able to discern in them a system of archetypes. In critical language the term 'archetype' refers to characters, settings or actions that recur over a range of literary works, and form a symbolic pattern that expresses submerged fears and tensions existing in society at large. These archetypal images can be related to the images of dreams, since they reflect preoccupations of which the writers themselves may be unconscious; the pattern made up by the interrelationship of the archetypes constitutes a literary myth.

A brief summary of the plot of *The Castle of Otranto*, which introduced the main archetypal figures and actions of the Gothic myth, should indicate what is meant here, and should also begin to shed some light on *Wuthering Heights*. The protagonist, Duke Manfred, is a cruel tyrant with a dark past, having usurped the Castle of Otranto. He conceives an incestuous desire for his intended daughter-in-law, the beautiful and virtuous Isabella, and pursues the terrified girl through the passages and caverns of the 'labyrinth of darkness' that is his castle. He fails to achieve his desires, and instead unintentionally kills his own daughter, the angelic Matilda. This terrible event comes after a number of supernatural signs and events that indicate Manfred's guilt; it brings about his conversion, and he resigns the castle to its rightful heir.

The Gothic protagonist, then, is a sinister tyrant, dark and demonic, and impelled by inhuman cruelty; he is often explicitly associated with the satanic, and there is usually a mystery about him related to his past. He has contempt for all conventional forms of authority, for the Church, the law, the privileges of rank and class. He is associated with an edifice that mirrors his character, a place of dark corners, of subterranean labyrinths, and he operates in a grim and hostile landscape that echoes the emotions that he himself arouses and that is littered with remnants of the past: old men, ruined churches, ruined castles. His persecution of established society and its values is indiscriminate as he seeks to gain absolute power, but his main victim, whom he pursues and imprisons, is a woman, fair-haired and beautiful, who embodies all the positives of her society. The emotional and spiritual turmoil of the atmosphere is intensified by dreams or nightmares and by intrusions of the supernatural.

The pattern here may seem to indicate a simple struggle between good and evil, a version of Satan's attempt to infiltrate and destroy the Garden of Eden, but there is something more, for it implies doubts about the power and validity of the authority that governs the Eden that it describes. The hierarchies of traditional Christian societies are justified by God's authority; the Gothic myth expresses a profound unease about the abilities of the established hierarchy of late-eighteenth-century England to withstand new pressures being brought to bear upon them. The Gothic protagonist embodies the energies of an individualism that sets itself against the values of established authority, which, if seen from his point of view, are repressive or obsolete. So although he is frequently described as satanic, he is related not so much to the Satan of the Bible as to the romantic interpretation of the Satan of Milton's *Paradise Lost*. Milton's Satan is a complex mixturê of envy and aspiration, of pride and suffering, and many readers find him attractive. This, no doubt, was Milton's intention, since it is the very attractiveness of evil that makes it dangerous, but depending upon your attitude towards authority, his Satan can be seen as attractive for different reasons: as the first revolutionary, heroically attempting to overthrow a repressive power, and harshly punished for it. The Gothic protagonist, sharing this aspect of Satan, consequently generates a certain amount of sympathy, in spite of his aggression and destructiveness (which is why he is sometimes referred to as a 'hero-villain'). What this myth appears to reflect is an unease in the writers with the ideals of Church and State put forward by the established order. The writers (reflecting a more widespread social unease) perceived the inadequacy of such reassuring ideals to solve the problems of repression and injustice.

By the middle of the nineteenth century, when Emily

Brontë wrote her tormented novel, the fears expressed in the Gothic had not been dissipated, and a variation of the Gothic myth can clearly be discerned in *Wuthering Heights*. Heathcliff contains all the archetypal resonances of the Gothic hero-villain. He is dark-haired, dark-skinned, dark-eyed. His origins are a mystery. The vocabulary used to define him consistently relates him to the diabolic: 'devil', 'goblin', 'imp of Satan', 'ghoul', he is 'a lying fiend, a monster, and not a human being', his eyes are 'the clouded windows of hell'. This, however, is how he is perceived by other characters; their language indicates their moral judgement, clouded by their own incomprehension of his energy, and does not necessarily imply a similar moral judgement on the part of the author. Indeed, a rather different interpretation of Heathcliff is suggested when he is first introduced into the Earnshaw household (he is significantly referred to as 'it', as if he were something indefinable), for Mr Earnshaw says of him 'you must e'en take it as a gift of God; though it's as dark almost as if it came from the devil' (chapter 4). Apart from Catherine, no one takes Heathcliff as a gift of God, but perhaps the novel is warning us here not to be taken in by over-simple judgements.

If we return to the rebellious satanic original to whom Heathcliff is related through the Gothic archetype, we see that although in an absolute sense his evil cannot be denied, he can nevertheless be seen as the first sufferer, a self-created outsider punished for his rebellion against God by extreme loss (of heaven) which fails to make him change his attitude, or to feel guilt or remorse for what he has done. This more sympathetic view of the satanic is echoed in a number of descriptions of Heathcliff; for example, when he returns to Wuthering Heights after his great loss (of Catherine), and prepares to embark on his revenge upon those he considers to be his enemies, Nelly Dean says of him, 'though his exterior was altered, his mind was unchangeable, and unchanged' (chapter 10). Again, when all is over, Heathcliff says to Nelly, 'as to repenting of my injustices, I've done no injustice, and I repent of nothing' (chapter 34). A mind that cannot change, that sees no injury in what it has performed, and yet constantly broods upon its own injuries, is a profoundly isolated mind, and can certainly create its own hell, as Heathcliff's does, and a realisation of this gives great force to Cathy's words to Heathcliff near to the end of the book: 'Mr Heathcliff, *you* have *nobody* to love you; and, however miserable you make us, we shall still have the revenge of thinking that your cruelty arises from your greater misery! You *are* miserable, are you not? Lonely, like the devil, and envious like him? *Nobody* loves you — *nobody* will cry for you, when you die! I wouldn't be you!' (chapter 29). Cathy, of course, has good reason to hate Heathcliff, but her words remind us that what may be hated may also be pitied, and this is the source of the ambiguity of our response to the Gothic hero-villain.

The Gothic protagonist is associated with a house of dark places, forbidding and prison-like, and this is certainly what Wuthering Heights is like when Heathcliff has control of it. We may note the similarity between Lockwood's descriptions of Heathcliff and the house in chapter 1: 'I beheld his black eyes withdraw so suspiciously under their brows'; 'The narrow windows are deeply set in the wall, and the corners defended with large jutting stones.' The inhospitableness of Heathcliff and his house ensures that neither Lockwood nor Isabella can find a comfortable resting place there; it is a place of torment for Hindley, and a prison for Cathy. Its name associates it with stormy turbulence, and its setting mirrors the distortion of Heathcliff's nature: 'One may guess the power of the north wind, blowing over the edge, by the excessive slant of a few stunted firs at the end of the house; and by a range of gaunt thorns all stretching their limbs one way, as if craving alms of the sun' (chapter 1). It is no accident that Heathcliff uses the same image when he reveals his plan to distort Hareton's spirit as he believes his has been distorted: 'Now, my bonny lad, you are *mine*! And we'll see if one tree won't grow as crooked as another, with the same wind to twist it!' (chapter 17).

This tendency to charge the landscape with emotions that echo those of the characters who populate it, a further characteristic of the Gothic, is one of the most notable features of *Wuthering Heights*. The grim and forbidding Yorkshire moors, hostile as they are to human activity ('a perfect misanthropist's heaven', Lockwood calls them), provide an ideal setting for a grim story, and in *Wuthering Heights* landscape and elements are usually described at moments of high emotional tension. Thus, when Heathcliff runs away, the night, even though it is summer, is wild and stormy: 'About midnight, while we still sat up, the storm came rattling over the Heights in full fury. There was a violent wind, as well as thunder, and either one or the other split a tree off at the corner of the building; a huge bough fell across the roof, and knocked down a portion of the east chimney-stack, sending a clatter of stones and soot into the kitchen fire.' (chapter 9). Similar effects are presented throughout the novel, for example at the death of Mr Earnshaw and at the flight of Isabella from Heathcliff, and, most notably, at the death of Heathcliff, when the elements pour in upon him in the haunted bedroom.

This identification of landscape with character, and particularly of Heathcliff with the wilder aspects of nature, reaches its most extreme in two attempts to define the difference between Heathcliff and Edgar. The first is Nelly's: 'The contrast resembled what you see in exchanging a bleak, hilly, coal country for a beautiful fertile valley' (chapter 8). The second is Catherine's attempt to describe her feelings about the two men: 'My love for Linton is like the foliage in the woods. Time will change it, I'm well, aware as winter changes the trees. My love for Heathcliff resembles the eternal rocks beneath — a source of little visible delight, but necessary'. (chapter 9). Note that this is not a simple contrast between positive and negative, as Nelly makes it seem — Catherine's image makes it clear that the harsher landscape has the more permanent value.

The other major symbolic figure of the Gothic is the persecuted maiden. She is the opposite of the protagonist, light where he is dark, the embodiment of the feminine principles of civilisation, of gentleness, of spirituality. At first sight it may seem that none of the women in *Wuthering Heights* fills this role; gentleness and spirituality are hardly their characteristics. Isabella and Cathy Linton both have the fair-haired beauty of the archetype, though Catherine Earnshaw has brown hair, her darkness perhaps indicating her likeness to Heathcliff. What is more important here, however, is that they are all persecuted by Heathcliff when he sees them as representatives of the cultivated established society that he hates. Thus, although Catherine is fundamentally so much like Heathcliff that she can identify herself with him, it is when she is seduced by the attractions of the Lintons' sophistication that she begins to separate herself from him, and when she apparently embraces these values by marrying Linton that Heathcliff begins his persecution of her. It is the same civilisation that he attacks when he marries Isabella in order to degrade her; and when he burns Cathy's books (we are told that he never reads) he is burning emblems of the past and of the culture that is rooted in the past.

It is here, really, that we can locate the central tension of the Gothic. It pits a new individualism, cut off from the past (and we note again that Heathcliff has no known past) against the authoritarian values of established society. Thus, although there may be a sexual element to it, the main reason for the protagonist's persecution of the maiden is that she embodies the values he hates. And our sympathy with him will depend, to a large degree, on whether that authority is presented as being of questionable value or, even, as being repressive. In *Wuthering Heights* the ideals of hierarchy and order presented by established society are indeed held up for questioning. Orthodox religion in the novel has degenerated to a point where it is represented on the one hand by the hypocritical and superstitious Joseph, and on the other by the dilapidated and untenanted chapel. For Joseph, 'the wearisomest, self-righteous Pharisee that ever ransacked a Bible to rake the promises to himself, and fling the curses to his neighbours' (chapter 5), religion is an instrument for his sadism, a means of triumphing over his enemies, a thing not of love or mercy, but of anxiety and fear. And almost the last image of the book is Lockwood's vision of the church in continued decline: 'When beneath its walls, I perceived decay had made progress, even in seven months — many a window showed black gaps deprived of glass; and slates jutted off, here and there, beyond the right line of the roof, to be gradually worked off in coming autumn storms' (chapter 34).

Civilised society is represented by the Lintons and Thrushcross Grange. Their superior class is reflected in the crimson and gold opulence of their household, and their consistent treatment of Heathcliff as an inferior, 'quite unfit for a decent house' (chapter 6). They embody the law (both Edgar and his father are magistrates), but it is clearly an ineffectual law against Heathcliff, who either ignores it, or manipulates it (by buying the services of Mr Green). Indeed, the implication of the novel is that the civilisation represented by the Lintons is degenerate; our first glimpse of them, seen amidst great opulence through Heathcliff's eyes, shows Edgar and Isabella fighting over a dog: 'And now, guess what your good children were doing? Isabella . . . lay screaming at the farther end of the room, shrieking as, if witches were running red-hot needless into her. Edgar stood on the hearth weeping silently, and in the middle of the table sat a little dog shaking its paw and yelping, which, from their mutual accusations, we understood they had nearly pulled in two between them.' (chapter 6). The irony of that 'your good children' is not merely Heathcliff's, for the characteristics of these two, who are to be victimised by Heathcliff, will remain constant through the book — Isabella foolishly wilful and self-centred, Edgar effete and weak.

Where Heathcliff sets himself up most completely against established values is in his attack on the great Victorian symbol of social harmony and respect for authority, the patriarchal family. An orphan himself, he has no father-figure of his own, and those he encounters in the book either abdicate or abuse responsibility. Mr Earnshaw, however well-meant his intentions, initiates the whole conflict of the novel by allowing Heathcliff to replace Hindley in his affections. Hindley himself, when he becomes the authority-figure in the Earnshaw family, is incapable of rational treatment of the son whom he apparently loves: 'he deserves flaying alive for not running to welcome me, and for screaming as if I were a goblin. Unnatural cub, come hither! I'll teach thee to impose on a good-hearted, deluded father . . . Hush, child, hush! well, then, it is my darling! wisht, dry thy eyes — there's a joy; kiss me; what! it won't? kiss me, Hareton! Damn thee, kiss me! By God, as if I would rear such a monster! As sure as I'm living, I'll break the brat's neck.' (chapter 9). Heathcliff himself consciously becomes a 'bad' father-figure with the express intention to 'demolish the two houses' of Earnshaw and Linton — to explode, that is, the notion of the family.

Wuthering Heights is not a Gothic novel, but it is clear that Emily Brontë has taken for her own purposes the Gothic's central submerged issue — of a society in conflict with its own past. She uses the Gothic structure to confront a disturbing question: if the authoritarian values of the past are obsolete or repressive, what can replace them to prevent the eruption of irrationality and chaos, the anarchy that Heathcliff's individualism implies? Perhaps there is no answer to the question, but it is a question that established society must face. It is no accident that the telling of Heathcliff's story is initiated in chapter 3 through curiosity aroused by the haunted dream of the novel's most 'civilised' character, Mr Lockwood, and that the horrible act of cruelty against the dream-child ('terror made me cruel; and finding it useless to attempt shaking the creature off, I pulled its wrist on to the broken pane, and rubbed it to and fro till the blood ran down and soaked the bedclothes') comes not from the tyrant Heathcliff, but from the unconscious depths of the mind of this civilised man. The terrors of *Wuthering Heights*, that is, are the terrors that civilisation is designed to suppress.

Faced directly, the incidents of *Wuthering Heights* and their implications might be too deeply disturbing, or might be laughed off as hyperbole and fantasy. The writers of Gothic novels placed their nightmares in remote or imaginary lands, distancing them, partly to give them credibility, partly to reassure their readers that these events were far from their real lives. *Wuthering Heights* is set in a very real, very concrete Yorkshire location, and has to be distanced in another way, displaced by being filtered through a framework of narrators. The conclusion too — allowing civilisation back into the world by having Cathy reclaim Hareton Earnshaw, and restoring him to the Wuthering Heights owned in 1500 by another Hareton Earnshaw, while giving him also the gentler Thrushcross Grange — reassures us that the 'real' world still operates. But after we put down the novel, what retains its hold on the imagination is that strange monster, that hero-villain Heathcliff, who threatens all of us, and is a part of all of us.

AFTERTHOUGHTS

1

What 'archetypes' (page 51) of the Gothic novel does Hyland identify in *Wuthering Heights*?

2

What explanations are offered in this essay for the rise of 'the Gothic myth' (page 52)?

3

'*Wuthering Heights* is not a Gothic novel' (page 57): what sort of a novel *is* it?

4

Compare Hyland's analysis of the social tensions present in the novel with Holderness's essay on pages 79–86.

Douglas Brooks-Davies

Douglas Brooks-Davies is Senior Lecturer in English Literature at the University of Manchester, and the author of numerous critical studies.

ESSAY

Characters, ghosts, and the margins of *Wuthering Heights*

As, in chapter 3, the snow embraces the farmhouse of Wuthering Heights in its whiteness, Lockwood reads a fragment of Catherine's diary which is written in the margins of a religious tract. Later in the same chapter he is visited by the ghost of Catherine who, as a waif — homeless, neglected, a wandering outcast — has existed for many years on the margins of the Heights, exiled like some strange female Cain (Genesis 4:14). In chapter 3 she comes out of the snow which, I suggest in this essay, seems to relate symbolically to the white margins in which, all those years before, she inscribed her secret thoughts. In the pages that follow I will concentrate largely on the third chapter, trying to tease out from it some of the literal and metaphorical implications of margins and marginality for the novel.

The heart of *Wuthering Heights* is Catherine's and Heathcliff's love for each other. Their union in childhood, their subsequent yearning for each other before and after Catherine's death, their oneness at the end — these are the core of the novel, its mysterious centre. As with many mysteries, however, it is possible to approach this one provided we observe the rituals. Our problem as readers is to discover what those rituals are and how they are to be observed, and thus proceed from the peripheries (or margins) to somewhere at least near the centre. In acknowledgement of the problem we are given Lockwood, image of all of us in his bafflement and irritation as he encounters riddle upon riddle in his approach to the Heights. But Lockwood gives up after chapter 3, handing the narrative over to Nelly who has more stamina and considerably more insight. Yet he returns at the end (chapter 32), so that Nelly's narrative is enclosed within the frame of Lockwood's own diary, and is thus central to the chronological margins with which he makes the novel's boundaries '1801' and, in chapter 32, '1802'.

Within Nelly's enclosed narrative are images of further enclosure — the two houses, the closet bed, the door which Lockwood tries to burst open, windows which are looked into. Yet each centripetal image is answered by a centrifugal one: flight from one or the other house; doors opened to permit egress; windows which are gazed longingly out of, as Catherine does in her last illness. In other words, the novel explores the fundamental paradox that opposites tread the same path, that when it comes to trying to understand a mystery distinctions disappear. And so in *Wuthering Heights* ghosts and visions tell the truth. Their world of above and beyond, marginal to the everyday world of waking phenomena, is in fact spiritually central and we are marginal to it.

Two main clues to this mystery, which take us back eventually to Lockwood in chapter 3, can be found in chapters 12 and 16. In the latter, Catherine gives birth to baby Cathy and dies shortly after. The baby is born almost exactly halfway through the novel at midnight, the hour when ghosts traditionally walk. When Heathcliff begs the dead Catherine to haunt him, to 'be with me always — take any form' (chapter 16), the baby maintains her 'constant wail' (chapter 17), just like the ghost in chapter 3 ('still it wailed, "Let me in!"') and like her mother in chapter 12: 'our fiery Catherine was no better than a wailing child!' In chapter 12 also Catherine gazes into a mirror. With her baby inside her she looks at her reflection, again at midnight: '"There's nobody here!" I insisted. "It was *yourself*, Mrs Linton; you knew it a while since." "Myself!" she gasped, "and the clock is striking twelve! It's true, then, that's dreadful!"' (chapter 12).

She thinks she has detected a premonition of her own death

in this ghostly absence, and in a way she has. For this riddle of a ghost story breaks all conventions of chronological linearity here in order to assert the total mystery that is Catherine. She *is* her baby ('Give over that baby-work'; 'wailing child') and her baby is her, and both are the wailing child of a ghost whom we meet in chapter 3, that chapter near the beginning of the novel which narrates events which are chronologically so much later than those recounted by Nelly at its centre. Emily Brontë's definition of Catherine in terms of her inner and outer and eternal 'self' (which, of course, also includes Heathcliff: 'I *am* Heathcliff — he's always in my mind ... as my own being' — (chapter 9) overthrows chronology in an attempt to capture her mystical essence because the world of the spirit, like that of the human unconscious, does not know time. Hence Catherine as mother and wailing baby; hence chapter 3 before chapter 12 but 'really' after it, while chapter 12 encloses a memory of Catherine in her closet bed that takes us back in time to the moment intruded on by Lockwood when, in that same bed in chapter 3, he opens Catherine's diary-in-the-margins and begins to read (compare this moment with chapter 12's: 'I was enclosed in the oak-panelled bed at home ... I was a child; my father was just buried ...' which remembers the moment written in the diary read by Lockwood). Catherine is simultaneously inner (her baby within her womb) and outer (her image in the glass, her own ghost the 'wrong' side of window) and, as child then mother then her own child, at once her past, present, and future selves, a secular embodiment of Christ's logic-defeating and breathtaking 'Before Abraham was, I am' (John 8:58).

In confirmation of this spatio-temporal riddle, as we approach the centre of the novel and the moment of Catherine's birth as ghost and baby, we are returned once more to chapter 3. Catherine has pulled handfuls of feathers from her pillow and Nelly exclaims: 'Lie down and shut your eyes, you're wandering. There's a mess! The down is flying about like snow!' (chapter 12). Verbal ambiguity (*down*, and *wandering*, which makes it seem as if Catherine is already a ghost) adds to our vertiginous sense of puzzlement as, bearing in mind Lockwood's south of England accent and vocabulary, we connect 'down ... like snow' with the snow-covered moors that trap Lockwood at the Heights for his reading of Catherine's marginalia and his dreams. What, then, actually happens in chapter 3?

It marks the last occasion, until the end at any rate, when Lockwood is our narrator. After it he hands over to Nelly Dean, that 'regular gossip' (chapter 4). The main meaning of 'gossip' at the time was godparent, baptismal sponsor. Lockwood chooses his word carefully, announcing that it is Nelly who now assumes responsibility and answers for, even enters into spiritual kindred with, the narrative. The fact that she takes over the narrative suggests a failure on his part, a failure that is identified in chapter 3.

Chapter 3 narrates Lockwood's enforced stay as the snow, minimal when he set out for the Heights, thickens into a storm so that he is prevented from returning to the Grange until morning. Even then he needs a guide because hollows have been filled in, mounds obliterated, and marker stones covered, so that all that can be seen in this 'billowy, white ocean' is 'a dirty dot pointing up, here and there' (chapter 3). This image is striking and a remarkably textual one if we think about it in connection with that self-consciously 'authorly' moment earlier on the same page when Heathcliff 'employ[s] an epithet as harmless as duck, or sheep, but generally represented by a dash', which enables us to supply the word while inviting us to meditate on the relationship between language and sign and print and social linguistic codes. If a dash can signify a word, then maybe dirty dots in the snow are analogues to the printed marks that stain the whiteness of the novel's pages and to the marks — those 'faded hieroglyphics' that comprise Catherine's diary in the margins of her despised religious books.

For Emily Brontë to draw attention to the nature of written and printed signs in this way is to invite speculation on the problems of interpretation, and this seems to be the function of the third chapter as a whole, in which Lockwood sets fire to a book (*the* Book, a Bible!), nods drowsily over another one, and is accused by the Reverend Jabes Branderham of failing to attend to his own mammoth exposition of a particular biblical text. As Lockwood reads and dreams in the closet bed inside a house which stands out blackly from the surrounding snow, the snow covers the marker stones to turn them into dots. Those dots are the residual signs of guide posts, reaching down far below the surface. As such they are like Catherine's marginalia, her writing in the blank whiteness left by the printer. The marks she has left tell a story which reaches down into the depths of her being.

This, then, is what Lockwood is invited, and fails, to realise: that the marks made by print and handwriting are cultural and psychological pointers, as deeply rooted in the collective and individual psyche as the marker stones are in the snow. As it is, however, he does make one astute remark in this chapter: that Catherine's writing is 'a pen and ink commentary — at least the appearance of one'. For this permits him (and us) to have it both ways, to see the diary as an independent text written coincidentally in the margins of religious texts and, simultaneously, to see it written in the margins of those texts as an implicit symbolic commentary on them, juxtaposing its rebellious life-force against the repressive Calvinistic code that the texts purvey and asserting thereby the wilfully Cain-like outsiderness (marginality) of Catherine's and Heathcliff's stance. The second is, of course, the truer reading. Catherine's diary fragment, which is at once the most chronologically distant and the most authentic presentation of her in the novel (because we are hearing her own thoughts as she wrote them unmediated by Nelly or anyone else) is, paradoxically marginal. But it is marginal to texts which encapsulate Joseph's Calvinism with its language of reprobacy, its eagerness to name people as outcast from God. To be marginal to that religious creed is, in the looking-glass language of *Wuthering Heights*, to be central.

If we now turn to the opening of chapter 3 we discover several more clues to the nature of Catherine's centrality in the way the window ledge leads Lockwood to the marginal script she left behind her:

> The ledge, where I had placed my candle, had a few mildewed books piled up in one corner; and it was covered with writing scratched on the paint. This writing, however, was nothing but a name repeated in all kinds of characters, large and small — *Catherine Earnshaw*; here and there varied to *Catherine Heathcliff*, and then again to *Catherine Linton*.
>
> In vapid listlessness I leant my head against the window, and continued spelling over Catherine Earnshaw — Heathcliff

— Linton, till my eyes closed; but they had not rested five minutes when a glare of white letters started from the dark, as vivid as spectres — the air swarmed with Catherines. . .

The ledge, below the window which overlooks the expanse of snowy moor, is written on, an inscribed margin to the window's blank page which Catherine will possess, appearing at its centre as her image appears in the mirror in chapter 12. When she appears she will tap with her hand and then, denied by Lockwood, will begin scratching as, all those years before, she scratched her name on the ledge. The ghost's scratching directs attention to the existence of Catherine as a spiritual being and the contrast between that denied essence and the Catherines conveyed by the scratched writing.

Yet it is not nearly as simple as that, for we note how the pun on *characters* (letters, and the character Catherine signified by those letters) prompts us to consider how in any fictional text people (characters) are created out of linguistic and typographical signs and to speculate on how this in turn links up with the diary 'scratched in an unformed childish hand', later designated by the technical term manuscript (from Latin *manus* + *scriptum*, handwriting): 'my eye wandered from manuscript to print' (chapter 3).

Print in this instance is the text of the religious book which Catherine counters by inscribing this fragment of her diary in its margins. The Catherine of the margins here becomes, in that dizzying reversal of everyday logic that characterises this novel, Catherine beyond the window, marginal to Wuthering Heights but central as a ghostly image framed by that window. Her scratching hand mimes her own action of writing the diary and Emily Brontë's in producing with her scratching pen letters which generated the living and unique characters of *Wuthering Heights*. There *is* a disparity between written and/or printed signs and the character and spirit that those signs are attempting to signify. But the *ledge* itself, with a pun on Latin *legi* (to read), merely invites us to read and in doing so to forget riddles and difficulties and concentrate on what these characters can do, which is to emphasise *Catherine* (who remains the constant element amid the shifting surnames), the essence of the character Catherine signified by the characters comprising the name Catherine.

This is our (and Lockwood's) most significant clue to reading Wuthering Heights (and *Wuthering Heights*): the mystery by which its secret — that extraordinary being which is Catherine — can be conveyed by writing. But the Lockwood who froze off the girl who liked him so much ('I was head over ears; she understood me, at last, and looked a return . . . and what did I do? I confess it with shame — shrank icily into myself, like a snail, at every glance retired colder and farther' — chapter 1) is not likely to want to follow this clue through to its end, which is confrontation with ghostly Catherine in all her otherness, that frozen waif who is at once herself and Heathcliff, female and male, and thus (to use the terms pioneered by the psychologist Jung) *anima* and *animus* together, female soul and male soul. This Catherine is a projection of the psychological reality of each of us because (and it was not merely Jung who argued this but Emily Brontë's romantic predecessors from Blake to Shelley, who were in turn influenced by Plato) we each contain and embody our sexual opposite. So Lockwood responds by trying to amputate the ghost's hand and in doing so to erase that other hand — Emily Brontë's — which wrote him, Catherine, Heathcliff, and all the others into their painful being as characters in the first place.

But Lockwood's death-wish on that tapping, scratching hand has already been partly frustrated by his own hypnotised imagination 'when a glare of white letters started from the dark, as vivid as spectres — the air swarmed with Catherines'. Catherine is mystically one and many, *vivid* (alive) to those close to their dream, as opposed to their rational waking, self. More than that, being our other, our opposite, she is not just on the margins and central simultaneously but a character who signifies the utter reversal of everyday norms. Hence she turns the page Lockwood is looking at into a photographic negative (white on dark).

At the very moment when these letters impinge on Lockwood's imagination, however, and his candle is illuminating the scene, he is thrown onto the margins of comprehension again. For these letters starting from the darkness turn him into Belshazzar, the King of Babylon who sees the writing on the wall in Daniel 5: 'In the same hour came forth the fingers of a man's hand, and wrote over against the candlestick upon the plaster of the wall'.

This writing is sent from God to announce Belshazzar's moral and spiritual failure and consequent imminent death: 'God hath numbered thy kingdom. . . . Thou art weighed in the balances and found wanting . . .'. And Belshazzar is king of confusion, which is the meaning of *Babylon* because it was built alongside and incorporates the name of the tower of Babel which was erected by Nimrod and others in an attempt to reach the heaven from which they were excluded by the Fall. God views the tower and destroys it, scattering its builders and causing the 'one language, and . . . one speech' which had prevailed until then to be confounded 'that they may not understand one another's speech' (Genesis 11:1,7).

Belshazzar's kingdom thus represents linguistic loss and it supplied western Europe with an enduring myth, one which was particularly alive in the first two decades of the nineteenth century when English romantic and other theorists were preoccupied with the origins of the language and the possibility of a primal language that survived in, for example, the speech of the peasantry. As explained by Wordsworth in the Preface to the *Lyrical Ballads* (1800; 1802) it comprises a purified version of the language of rustics infused with the intuitive utterance of children which ideally transcends boundaries of species, gender, and death: Johnny's 'The cocks did crow to-whoo, to-whoo' in *The Idiot Boy* and the little girl's insistence that 'we are seven' in the poem of that name, for instance.

Belshazzar, king of linguistic confusion, cannot read the writing on the wall; and Lockwood, like him, cannot in the end make sense of the writing that stares from the ledge (interestingly, Charlotte Brontë used the story as a parable for critics of *Wuthering Heights* itself in her 'Biographical Notice' to the 1850 edition of the novel). He embraces the world of babble, of words for the sake of words, because words function for him as barriers to intuitive understanding. Ever on the margins of *Wuthering Heights*, he is at home with books but not with books whose characters become vivid and yield ghosts who demand entrance to the core of his being.

Refusing Catherine, then, Lockwood turns his back on the Heights and follows the dirty dots through the snow to Thrushcross where he requests a story from his housekeeper. This story is, of course, *Wuthering Heights*, a long commentary on and explanation of Catherine's diary written in the margins of now mildewed books. But it can perform no more than the swarming Catherines and the scratching hand did to disclose the novel's secret because they are its secret. In a way a Daniel to Lockwood's Belshazzar (her name almost seems to be a reversal of Dan-niel's), Nelly Dean does not so much interpret as repeat the riddles of chapter 3, weaving a multiplicity of words around them in order to satisfy Lockwood in his confusion. There is one occasion, though, when she reveals their meaning in the most explicit way possible. It occurs at the beginning of chapter 11 when she narrates how she paused before a marker stone and scrutinised its letters:

> I came to a stone where the highway branches off on to the moor at your left hand; a rough sand-pillar, with the letters W. H. cut on its north side, on the east, G., and on the south-west, T. G. It serves as a guide-post to the Grange, and Heights, and village.
>
> The sun shone yellow on its grey head, reminding me of summer; I cannot say why, but all at once, a gush of child's sensations flowed into my heart. Hindley and I held it a favourite spot twenty years before.
>
> I gazed long at the weather-worn block; and, stooping down, perceived a hole near the bottom . . . and, as fresh as reality, it appeared that I beheld my early playmate seated on the withered turf . . .

Cheated by her 'bodily eye' she stares at him, rushes to the Heights, and makes the apparition turn into Hareton ('it stood looking through the gate') and then into Heathcliff ('Heathcliff appeared . . . and I . . . ran down the road as hard as ever I could race, making no halt till I gained the guide-post, and feeling as scared as if I had raised a goblin'). In other words, Nelly has no difficulty turning letters into characters, in conjuring up and communing with living spectres.

The meaning of the novel on this level is that 'faded hieroglyphics' require us as readers to transform them into vivid characters. Chapter 3 and Nelly's stone thus point us to the end of the novel where Lockwood, pausing by the tombstones, 'watched the moths fluttering among the heath and hare-bells;

listened to the soft wind breathing through the grass; and wondered how anyone could ever imagine unquiet slumbers, for the sleepers in that quiet earth'. For tombstones are themselves marker stones, registering our transition from known to unknown, and recording initials, names, and dates. They demand that we turn their inscribed characters into vivid characters through acts of memory (if we knew the dead people) or (if we did not) through acts of sympathetically imaginative story-weaving.

Once more, as with the ice-cold hand, Lockwood fails as, indeed, does Nelly if we take her 'I believe the dead are at peace' in its conventional pietistic sense. Being Nelly, though, and belonging to the world of the Heights as she does, she also knows the truth and acknowledges it at the moment she denies it. Of the shepherd boy who has seen 'Heathcliff, and a woman, yonder, under t'Nab', she says: 'He probably raised the phantoms from thinking . . . on the nonsense he had heard his parents and companions repeat'. Raising phantoms is transforming characters into vivid spectres, recognising and acknowledging spirits, making Catherine, with all the others, and Emily Brontë as well, live through our act of reading.

Nelly's dismissive 'nonsense' and her 'the dead are at peace' are therefore less true to her perceptions, however flawed some of them may be, than her 'yet still, I don't like being out in the dark, now'. Indeed, they probably merely reflect her narrator's anxiety that her story should end, that she should close it with all the threads neatly tied. The same excuse cannot be made for Lockwood. He cannot *imagine* unquiet slumbers, cannot (except in that one moment of challenge in chapter 3 when he nodded on the threshold and passed his eyes over the ledge and Catherine's marginalia) raise phantoms by thinking, cannot, therefore, perceive the irony of his own returns (in the novel's opening sentence; to Thrushcross Grange at the end of chapter 3 as 'the clock chimed twelve'; to Thrushcross again at the beginning of chapter 32) in this novel of revenants. We are all ghostly (because spiritual) selves, but he refuses that knowledge. But then, this traveller, unlike Catherine's ghost, is the one character who is really on the margins of Wuthering Heights.

AFTERTHOUGHTS

1

In what different ways is the word 'margins' being used in the opening paragraph of this essay and in the argument as a whole?

What does Brooks-Davies mean on page 62 by 'she *is* her baby'?

3

Do you agree that Catherine's diary fragment is 'the most authentic presentation of her in the novel' (page 64)?

4

Explain the comparison that Brooks-Davies makes in this essay between Lockwood and Belshazzar (pages 66–67).

Kate Flint

Kate Flint is Fellow in English Literature at Mansfield College, Oxford and the author of numerous critical studies.

ESSAY

The return of the repressed: passion and violence in *Wuthering Heights*

In her preface to the 1850 edition of *Wuthering Heights*, Charlotte Brontë remarks on the 'harshly manifested passions' which, together with 'rough, strong utterances', she thinks might be a disquieting feature for a restrained and cultured audience. More particularly, she singles out among these passions Heathcliff's love for Catherine:

> a sentiment fierce and inhuman: a passion such as might boil and glow in the bad essence of some evil genius; a fire that might form the tormented centre — the ever-suffering soul of a magnate of the infernal world: and by its quenchless and ceaseless ravage effect the execution of the decree which dooms him to carry Hell with him wherever he wanders.

nice intro for someone's essay?

This description is as remarkable for what it reveals of Charlotte Brontë's own anxieties concerning the sources and consequences of sexual passion as it is for the analysis it offers of her sister's novel. Nonetheless, it serves to foreground the presence of passion, violence and desire within the text, and raises questions about their origin.

Charlotte Brontë goes on to ask whether or not it is right or advisable to create 'things' like Heathcliff. By this word, she dehumanises that diabolic being, yet immediately she suggests that there may be links between his uncompromising fierceness and Emily Brontë's own powers as a writer. Within creativity there may be an element of the uncontrollable: 'the writer who possesses the creative gift owns something of which he is not always master — something that at times strangely wills and works for itself'. Yet whilst violent passion and the anguish of unfulfilled desire are unmistakably central to *Wuthering Heights*, I want initially to show that the tendency of the text and its organisation is to display these disruptive emotions and then, ostensibly, to control them.

Above all, passion and desire — wanting, but not possessing — can be seen in the ineradicable bond between Heathcliff and Catherine. In chapter 9, Catherine tries to articulate this bond to Nelly, seeking validity for the intensity of her feelings by locating the object of her desire both within herself — 'he's more myself than I am' — and then in external nature, in 'the eternal rocks beneath — a source of little visible delight, but necessary': Heathcliff is the core, this imagery suggests, of her own stability and existence. Her attachment to Edgar Linton, sanctioned by social propriety, is, as we are to see, subject to change, and is perceived by Catherine, even at this stage, as being like 'the foliage in the woods'. Such language disquiets Nelly, since it indicates to her either that Catherine doesn't understand the full implications of her impending marriage to Edgar, or that she is wicked and unprincipled: remarks which Nelly does not explain. Yet despite the fact that the unimaginative, snobbish Nelly calls Catherine's illustrative imagery 'nonsense', she does nothing to question the younger woman's equation of deep emotional feelings with that which is simultaneously personal, natural, and illogical. Heathcliff runs away when he hears no more of Cathy's outburst than that it would degrade her to marry him. Brontë, in her turn, underlines the 'naturalness' of this by calling down a wild and destructive storm upon the Heights, which is both prophetic of future disturbance, and above all indicative of the novelist's implicit support for Catherine's frame of reference.

The representation of Heathcliff's behaviour after his

return shocked and perplexed contemporary reviewers. The book 'strongly shows the brutalizing influence of unchecked passion', wrote the *Britannia*'s critic. 'In *Wuthering Heights*, the reader is shocked, disgusted, almost sickened by details of cruelty, inhumanity, and the most diabolical hate and vengeance', claimed *Douglas Jerrold's Weekly Newspaper,* whilst the *North American Review* called Heathcliff a 'deformed monster'. Certainly, some scenes still shock now: that in which Heathcliff violently clasps the heavily pregnant Catherine to him as she complains bitterly of her emotional imprisonment, or that where Heathcliff describes his frenetic uncovering of her coffin, which results not in a sense of peace but of infernal torture from her persistently haunting presence. What makes the emotions so capable of disturbing the reader is the everyday context in which they are allowed to appear. Unlike scenes of horror in the Gothic novel of the late eighteenth and early nineteenth century, they are not distanced by taking place in a foreign country, against a background of Catholic superstition, and at a date significantly earlier than their time of composition. Despite the narrative which glances backwards into the eighteenth century, the date at the beginning of Lockwood's account (1801) sets the framework of the story's narration unmistakably in Emily Brontë's own century, during the Napoleonic wars — a period of political rather than metaphysical instability. Whilst Charlotte Brontë writes in her preface of the novel being hewn in a 'wild workshop', sculpted from 'a granite block on a solitary moor', the environment is hardly untouched by human activity: Lockwood, stumbling back from the Heights in the snow, has to take care not to fall into excavated pits or stumble over 'entire ranges of mounds, the refuse of the quarries' (chapter 3). Looking towards the moors, Emily Brontë had literally to turn her back on the Industrial Revolution: as the first chapter of Elizabeth Gaskell's *Life of Charlotte Brontë* shows, the road up to Haworth, the Brontë's home, was lined with worsted factories and industrialists' villas, the air 'dim and lightless with the smoke from all these habitations and places of business'. Heathcliff's origins are obscure. Coming from the rapidly growing port of Liverpool, he may be seen in the light of contemporary fears about the self-made man and his power to disrupt established family life and traditions. For Heathcliff's energy does not just derive from the uncontrollable fury of his passions and from the depth of his sense of loss, but from his ability both to understand the importance of property, and to manipulate the laws of entail: his diabolic power has a material as well as an emotional base.

Heathcliff's extremes of feeling and violent actions, both emotional and physical, are parallelled by instances of violence elsewhere. Thus it is implicitly suggested that Heathcliff's passions are not the product of one disturbed, diabolical individual, but may be inherent within many people — a worrying thought, indeed, at a time when anxiety about origins increasingly extended into the debate about evolution and the characteristics which were most likely to ensure the direction of the future development of the human race. Sometimes, these instances are, of course, directly related to Heathcliff, as when Isabella, escaped from the Heights, smashes her wedding ring with a poker — although Nelly deflates the violence done to this image of Heathcliff's bondage by calling Isabella's actions those of 'childish spite' (chapter 17). At other moments, what we see seems no more than commonplace and omnipresent brutality, as with Hindley's bullying of Heathcliff, his alarming flourishing of the combination of pistol and double-edged knife, or the moment when Nelly, escaping from the dinner knife Heathcliff hurls at her, 'knocked over Hareton, who was hanging a litter of puppies from a chairback' (chapter 17). Moreover, as Isabella's understandable histrionics here indicate, savage aggression is not limited to those with a boorish upbringing. That 'civilisation' may be no more than a veneer is brought home when Heathcliff and Catherine, as children, peep through the window of Thrushcross Grange, and, against a backcloth of crimson carpet and ornate chandelier, see two shrieking and weeping children, and the damaged, yelping dog which they had nearly pulled apart in their quarrel. There is an ominous undertone to Nelly's remark — when Lockwood tries to draw a distinction between life in town and country — 'Oh! here we are the same as anywhere else, when you get to know us' (chapter 7).

It is through Nelly's narrative, told via Lockwood, that Emily Brontë brings some semblance of order to these events. The doubling of narrators — plus Isabella's letter, and the scrap of Catherine's early writing — gives a sense of crafted organisation to the novel: an author who is in control, even if the passions of her created characters are not. This impression is heightened by the time-scheme, moving backward and forward in the course of the novel, gently interfolding past and present whenever Lockwood comes into contact with the Heights. Additionally, the novel is constructed according to neat patternings: one girl, one boy in both the original Earnshaw and Linton families, with Heathcliff the outsider who disrupts these pairings; one child resulting from each marriage, the second generation echoing, though not replicating, the characteristics of the first. Such deliberation in planning is reflected, too, in the careful speech and personal characteristics of the principal transmitters of the action: through the 'citified', literary Lockwood, and through Nelly, proud of her own capacity for social advancement by means of book learning, and almost complacent at her inability to be stirred by the events around her, going about 'my household duties, convinced that the Grange had but one sensible soul in its walls, and that lodged in my body' (chapter 12).

Yet Charlotte Brontë, in suggesting that there was in Emily something which she could not always 'master', picked up on the fact that the overall effect of reading *Wuthering Heights* is most certainly not that of a celebration of civilisation and order. The passionate outburst of Catherine to Nelly, the violence of Heathcliff gnashing and foaming like a mad dog, or dashing his head in grief against a tree-trunk, stick in the memory longer than the loving, playful slap which the young Cathy gives to Hareton as she teaches him to read. The happiness, indeed, which this young couple show at the end of the novel is not something on which Lockwood wishes to dwell. Whilst Lockwood's narrative neatly frames the book, the stirrings of his own unconscious are still at work. The glimpses which we receive of his inner life reveal how his desire to control and to order is in fact dependent on the repression and evasion of strong forces at work within the unconscious.

Nowhere is this more apparent than when, in chapter 3, we learn of his vivid dreams: dreams which he tries, vainly, to explain away as 'the effects of bad tea and bad temper'. Their sources, however, are otherwise. On the one hand, these dreams derive from Lockwood's bedtime reading: from the suggestivity of the title of the Reverend Jabes Branderham's sermon, glimpsed just as he slides into sleep, and, even more influentially, from the marginal scribblings of Catherine Earnshaw. But I would suggest that these immediate stimuli are related, additionally, to what Emily Brontë tells us of Lockwood's own past, notably his bolting from the sweet looks of his seaside companion, 'a most fascinating creature, a real goddess' which, as soon as it acknowledged the existence of Lockwood's sexual and emotional desire, ensured that he 'shrank icily into myself, like a snail' (chapter 1). Such acute repression of desire emerges, disturbingly, in his dream, when Lockwood enacts his revenge on forward womanhood: '"Let me in — let me in!"' . . . Terror made me cruel; and, finding it useless to attempt shaking the creature off, I pulled its wrist on to the broken pane, and rubbed it to and fro till the blood ran down and soaked the bedclothes.' (chapter 3). This dreamed incident has no function in the plot other than as a means to introduce the uncontrollable anguish of Heathcliff's sense of loss, and as a revelation of a fact never developed, that the mild and pedantic Lockwood has a potentially violent side to him.

Whether we like it or not, however, the structure of the novel brings us, the readers, closer to Lockwood than to any other character. The sensation of the strangeness of the moorland environment, the educative facts which are solemnly given us ('"Wuthering" being a significant provincial adjective, descriptive of the atmospheric tumult to which its station is exposed in stormy weather' (chapter 1) place us, like Lockwood, as visitors from the South. When at the end of chapter 1 we are told that despite Heathcliff evidently wishing no repetition of his intrusion, 'I shall go, notwithstanding', we may note Lockwood's peculiar obtuseness in human relations, but we, like him, are implicated in the wish to know more about the history of the uncouth inhabitants of the lonely farmhouse. Similarly, at the end of the novel, our desire for calmness and for a feeling of completion is pandered to by Lockwood's inability to conceive how 'anyone could ever imagine unquiet slumbers, for the sleepers in that quiet earth' (chapter 34). But, even if Catherine and Heathcliff have found rest, or oblivion, this fact does nothing to eliminate the presence of desire and its effects in everyday life. Lockwood feels only discomfort in the presence of the happy couple, the younger Catherine and Hareton: 'I felt irresistibly impelled to escape them again'. Desire can never be entirely controlled or repressed by what Charlotte Brontë calls, in her preface, 'rules and principles'. It is this perpetual presence which *Wuthering Heights* dramatises, and from which the novel draws its strength.

AFTERTHOUGHTS

1

Flint implies that Charlotte Brontë's comments on *Wuthering Heights* (page 71) tell us something about her own view of passion; in what ways does Emily Brontë's view differ?

2

What relationship between order and passion is identified in this essay?

3

Did any scenes in *Wuthering Heights* 'shock' *you* (page 73)?

4

Do you agree that we are brought 'closer to Lockwood than to any other character' in *Wuthering Heights* (page 76)?

Graham Holderness

Graham Holderness is Head of the Drama Department at the Roehampton Institute of Higher Education, and has published numerous books and critical articles, including a study of Wuthering Heights *(Open University Press, 1985).*

ESSAY

Class struggle in *Wuthering Heights*

> 'Having levelled my palace, don't erect a hovel and complacently admire your charity in giving me that for a home.'
>
> (chapter 11)

Emily Bronte's *Wuthering Heights* is known as a novel of intense and violent conflict. Conflict occurs within the book at several levels — human relationship, natural atmosphere, supernatural drama — and has thus been explained in several different ways — as conflicts of passion, of the elements, or of religious vision. One of the ways in which conflict is dramatically realised is in a continual emphasis on social and cultural *differences*, and on the conflicts that arise from, or are formulated in, historical or sociological terms.

From the opening pages in which Mr Lockwood, the southern dilettante, enters the bizarre and unfamiliar world of the remote northern farmhouse, the novel is constantly stressing these facts of difference. By using a conventional upper-class language ('while enjoying a month of fine weather at the sea-coast' (chapter 1)) that clashes violently against the rough dialect of the other characters and the harsh domestic atmosphere of the Heights, Lockwood marks himself out as both stranger and intruder. The meeting of landlord and tenant is a collision of two different and distinct social worlds: an independent, sociable city-dweller is introduced to the strange territory of an impenetrably bewildering social landscape.

Naturally he begins to make mistakes. He compliments Cathy on her 'favourites', only to discover that they are dead rabbits. He assumes that Cathy will display the amiable and hospitable manners familiar in the ladies of his own social milieu; but is swiftly disillusioned when she flings the teaspoon back into the caddy. He takes Hareton (in reality the true heir to the estate) to be a common labourer or servant because of his dress and manner, and gets entirely the wrong idea about the system of relationships at the Heights. By making these errors of judgement Lockwood marks out a social distance between himself and the community he is entering; and that distance begins to suggest that the violent conflicts that take place within the farmhouse have something to do with class.

The sharpest formulation of this cultural difference is made in the contrast between Wuthering Heights and Thrushcross Grange. In chapter 6 Heathcliff narrates the description that introduces us to the other house: with him we stare from outside at a scene of unprecedented richness, splendour and luxury, contrasting with the stark simplicity of domestic atmosphere at Wuthering Heights. When the children are detected, the Lintons react to an invasion from outside with the instincts of property-owners, assuming the strangers to be 'robbers', 'thieves' and 'rascals' (chapter 6), and using guns and dogs to protect themselves from imaginary enemies. Heathcliff is recognised immediately as a criminal type: 'the villain scowls so plainly in his face, would it not be a kindness to the country to hang him at once, before he shows his villany in acts as well as features?' (ibid.).

Catherine is accepted into the Grange and Heathcliff expelled. When she returns to the Heights she is transformed, from 'a hatless little savage' to 'a very dignified person' (chapter 7). 'You look like a lady now', says Hindley (ibid.): and it is as a *lady* (not an adult, but a member of a superior social class) that Catherine now appears, in dress, manners and social attitudes. Her dress is appropriate to the Grange rather than the Heights: 'she was obliged to hold up with both hands . . . a long cloth habit' (ibid.) — a cumbersome and clumsy style of dress for a farmhouse. Her fingers are 'wonderfully whitened with doing nothing, and staying indoors' (ibid.) — she has become accustomed to a world where life is centred on the inside of houses, and where, above all, she *does no work*. She has become accustomed to a style of living where class status and privilege place her above those who work for her, produce for her and support her needs; and where her dress, manners, speech and social attitudes separate her clearly from the inferior class. Heathcliff, dirty and neglected, finds himself constituted as a member of that inferior class, and resists by embracing the very signs of his oppression: 'I shall be as dirty as I please, and I like to be dirty, and I will be dirty' (ibid.).

The central action of the novel's plot, Catherine's decision to marry Edgar Linton rather than Heathcliff, is presented as very much a social choice. Edgar Linton 'will be rich, and I shall like to be the greatest woman of the neighbourhood, and I shall be proud of having such a husband' (chapter 9); whereas 'if Heathcliff and I married, we should be beggars' (ibid.). The consequent rivalry between Heathcliff, the dark stranger of uncertain origin, and Linton, gentleman and landowner, is frequently formulated in social terms, with the former subjected to social abuse as a 'gipsy' and 'ploughboy', and the latter resorting to the authority of his position in order to negotiate an unequal physical and spiritual contest. Heathcliff sees Catherine's preference for Linton as a form of class-oppression: 'Having levelled my palace, don't erect a hovel and complacently admire your own charity in giving me that for a home' (chapter 11).

These examples demonstrate conclusively that *Wuthering Heights* is in some way concerned with problems of social class, and that the violent conflicts which are, by common consent, characteristic of its artistic structure are to a degree expressed and formulated in terms of social conflict. This fact has naturally prompted readers and critics to seek for the roots and causes of this violence and conflict in the pressures of the historical society within which the novel was shaped.

Wuthering Heights was published in 1848. The historical period of its composition was a time of great economic change, industrial unrest and political instability, both in Britain and in Europe as a whole. The Brontë sisters grew up in the second phase of the Industrial Revolution, when the great inventions of the eighteenth century, such as power-driven machinery, were developed and consolidated into the factory system. The 1840s saw the growth of full-scale capitalism, with its accompanying cycles of boom and slump. The emergence of trade unionism in the 1830s, around the struggles against the Poor Law and for improved factory conditions, enabled class battles between organised labour and their employers to be conducted on a new, much larger scale. During the 1840s the rise of a broad democratic movement known as Chartism, aimed at campaigning for reform by mass meetings and demonstrations, provoked the government to severe policies of repression. The West Riding of Yorkshire was at the heart of all these changes and conflicts.

It is often believed that the Brontë sisters lived an isolated existence on the edge of the wild moors. Haworth, their home, was not in fact a remote country village but a small industrial town near Keighley, in the industrial West Riding of Yorkshire, near the centre of the woollen area. It was an expanding town, which grew in population between 1811 and 1831 from 3,971 to 5,835. There were worsted mills in Haworth, and the great events occurring in the large towns like Leeds and Bradford (and recorded in newspapers that went to Haworth parsonage) found their echo in the smaller industrial centres: there were strikes and lock-outs in Haworth too, in which the Reverend Patrick Brontë as the local clergyman was inevitably involved — at one time he incurred the anger of the local employers by assisting the locked-out workers of his parish. Nor was Emily Brontë confined to her home town: she visited Leeds, Bradford, Keighley, Halifax; even, for a short time, Brussels in Belgium. The turbulent world of mid-nineteenth-century historical events was thus completely open to her.

These two kinds of evidence — the presence in the novel of a preoccupation with social conflict, and the facts of social conflict in the novel's historical context — taken in combination may point us towards an apparently obvious conclusion: that *Wuthering Heights* in some way (more or less directly) reflects the class struggles that surrounded its original production. If this follows, then the conflicts we find in the novel — between Heathcliff and Linton, between Heights and Grange — may be regarded as symbolic of the struggles between the organised working classes and their bourgeois employers, the latter assisted by government and state. Heathcliff may be considered a symbolic representative of the nineteenth-century proletariat — propertyless, dirty with toil, rejected and victimised; but full of irrepressible energy, powerful determination and a 'wild endeavour to hold [his] right'. He becomes an embodiment and bearer of the values of social justice: his struggle against the Lintons a sustained effort to rectify the injustice of his own exploitation and dispossession.

Before proceeding to consider the problems presented by this argument for our interpretation of the novel, let us reflect on the general assumption underlying the argument itself: which is that a novel is bound to reflect more or less directly the economic and political conditions of its contemporary society.

The old cliché about Jane Austen's lack of interest in contemporary history shows that a novelist could, if she chose, simply ignore the great happenings (like the French Revolution or the Napoleonic Wars) that historians have designated as the significant events of her time. This does not mean that Jane Austen was not concerned with society or with social conflict: only that she chose to focus, not on the contradictions between classes, but on moral problems within a particular class, the landowning gentry. That concentration enabled her not only to achieve an intensity of focus, but also to present convincingly the ultimate resolution of the conflicts she dramatised. The world she was living in was a changing world, which would in time transform her class and remove it from political domination; but she wanted to present in her fiction images of a world in which change could always be contained, and could take place without destruction or subversion of a settled social order.

When we begin to investigate more closely the precise realisation of conflict in *Wuthering Heights*, a distance begins to appear between the kinds of social struggle we encounter when reading books about mid-nineteenth-century history, and the specific forms in which conflicts are dramatised in the fiction. The differences between Wuthering Heights and Thrushcross Grange, for example, are differences of *culture* rather than of class. The Earnshaw family is closer to the land and to agricultural labour; they could be described as a yeoman-farming family. The Lintons have constructed a distance between themselves and the rural economy: their house stands in a park, surrounded by a wall, a frontier between civilisation and the land or wild nature. The Heights has all the primitive roughness of a peasant life-style; the Grange the civilised luxury of an aristocratic society.

But these are differences of life-style, not economic, financial, political or class differences. The families are socially compatible, or at least of equal status. When the Lintons catch the children outside Thrushcross Grange, they make no distinction between them until Catherine is recognised as the daughter of a local landowner: it is on that basis that she is accepted into the house and the family. There is no disapproval on either side of a marriage alliance between the two households: an important index of social compatibility. When the second Catherine and Hareton marry at the end of the novel, uniting the families for the second time, they move naturally from the Heights to the Grange. The Heights could be described as representative of a more traditional or old-fashioned style of living for the same landowning class; just as in Jane Austen some gentry families adhere to the feudal institutions of their country estates, while others seek the social life of the city or town.

It is only the outsider Heathcliff, belonging to neither family, who introduces a real sense of social difference. The 'gipsy brat' old Mr Earnshaw brings home with him has neither name nor status, property nor possessions: a stranger who — unlike anyone else in the novel — has no proper and apportioned place in the social hierarchy. Heathcliff emerges from the darkness which is the *outside* of the tightly knit family system, and introduces an alien element into a jealously guarded system of parental and filial relations, of inheritance and possession. Hindley from the outset sees Heathcliff (correctly, in the event) as a rival for his own father's affections and his own position as heir, a potential disrupter of the ancient lineage.

Except for the fact that Heathcliff is apparently of proletarian origin, and is later reduced by Hindley from the family position bestowed on him by Mr Earnshaw to the status of a servant or labourer, it is hard to see this pattern as representative of the nineteenth-century struggles between working class and bourgeoisie. It is a struggle for power entirely within an ancient family of the landowning gentry. Furthermore, Heathcliff does not remain the victim of exploitation. He resolves to free himself from the humiliation of oppression by attaining for himself the status of an oppressor. His plan of revenge, carefully laid and executed, is to revenge himself on Hindley and the Lintons by two methods: exploiting their children in precisely the same way that Hindley and Edgar exploited him; and by expropriating their lands and possessions and seizing them himself. 'The tyrant grinds down his slaves', says Heathcliff, 'and they don't turn against him, they crush those beneath them' (chapter 11). That is not the philosophy of a proletarian revolutionary. Heathcliff may well be responsible for provoking and disclosing the latent violence and conflict within the gentry class; but he does so by engaging in an internal struggle for power and status with them, not by challenging their values or authority from a clearly defined alternative perspective.

Although Heathcliff and Catherine act out their tragic destiny, the concluding events of the novel show a pattern of resolution and reconciliation. When Mr Lockwood returns to Wuthering Heights after Heathcliff's death, he encounters certain changes: 'I had neither to climb the gate, nor to knock — it yielded to my hand. That is an improvement! I thought.' (chapter 32). Gates and doors previously locked are now open: flowers grow among the fruit trees. The cultural atmosphere of the house has moved away from the rough utilitarianism of the old farmstead, where a feudal defensiveness sought to exclude a hostile world. In a sense, the primitive culture of the Heights has moved closer to the sophisticated civilisation of the Grange.

A similar change is reflected in the relationship of Catherine and Hareton, which naturally invites comparison with the earlier relationship of Catherine and Heathcliff. Estrangement is replaced by friendship, conflict by sympathetic cooperation, anger and resentment by love. The story of Catherine and Heathcliff, a tale of tragic conflict and separation by family enmity, class, marriage and death, gives way to a narrative of reconciliation between Heights and Grange, Earnshaw and Linton, male and female. Hatred leads to love, conflict to mutual understanding, separation to union.

Thus we see that *Wuthering Heights* is not about the unresolved (and still, for some of us, unfinished) conflict between proletariat and bourgeoisie in the 1840s. It is about a conflict within a single class, the early-nineteenth-century landowning gentry; a conflict which is opened out into violent confrontation by the arrival of an alien outsider, but which proves ultimately to be capable of reconciliation and healing. Only on the margins of that resolution appear the unappeased forces of unreconciled desire — the ghosts of Catherine and Heathcliff may still be wandering the moors, suggesting by their disturbing restlessness that social conflicts are easier to pacify in fiction than they are in reality.

AFTERTHOUGHTS

1

What social conflicts does Holderness identify in the opening chapter of *Wuthering Heights?*

2

Do you agree with the assumption that 'a novel is bound to reflect more or less directly the economic and political conditions of its contemporary society' (page 83)?

3

What arguments does Holderness put for and against the suggestion that *Wuthering Heights* might symbolise 'the struggles between the organised working classes and their bourgeois employers' (pages 83–86)? Do you agree with his conclusion?

4

In what ways can Hyland's analysis on pages 52–58 of the social tensions in the novel be related to the argument of this essay?

Alan Gardiner

Alan Gardiner has been a GCE examiner for several years and is a Lecturer in English Language and Literature at Redbridge Technical College. He is the author of numerous critical studies.

ESSAY

Does the novel deteriorate after the death of Catherine?

The meticulous construction of *Wuthering Heights* has received much attention from critics. The novel is the story of two generations and Emily Brontë took pains to divide the book accordingly, giving to each generation a similar number of chapters. The purpose of this essay is to consider whether there is a corresponding consistency of artistic achievement. The greatness of the first half of the novel is widely acknowledged — but is this greatness sustained in the remainder of the book?

It is generally accepted that the later chapters are not a superfluous addition to the story but serve necessary structural and thematic purposes. The second generation of characters is in fact introduced at the very beginning of the novel, when Lockwood on his first visits to Wuthering Heights meets not only Heathcliff but also Hareton Earnshaw and the younger Catherine. He has Catherine in particular in mind when he asks Nelly to tell him more about the inhabitants of the Heights: 'that pretty girl-widow, I should like to know her history' (chapter 4). Interest in the second generation then recedes as

Nelly recounts the story of Heathcliff, the elder Catherine and Edgar Linton. But following Catherine's death, recounted midway through the novel (chapter 16), attention shifts to Hareton, young Cathy Linton and Linton Heathcliff, and it becomes apparent that the novel consists of two complementary parts. There are many similarities and contrasts between the two generations and these deepen our understanding of the characters and enhance our capacity to judge them. At the risk of over-simplifying the novel's complex pattern, it might be said that each Catherine experiences two kinds of love relationship, one with a man who is socially her inferior but with whom she is emotionally compatible, and another with a man who is socially advantaged but fundamentally dissimilar in temperament. The elder Catherine marries Edgar, rejecting Heathcliff because it would 'degrade' her to become his wife, whereas her daughter, though initially forced into marriage to Linton, decides after her husband's death to marry Hareton despite his deprived upbringing and lack of education. The parallels between the two halves of the novel enable us to see more clearly that the elder Catherine chose wrongly, and that young Cathy did right to accept Hareton. The characters of Hareton and Cathy, and the marriage between them, are also important because they represent a reconciliation between the hitherto conflicting worlds of Wuthering Heights and Thrushcross Grange. Hareton, although raised at Wuthering Heights and moulded as a child by Heathcliff, comes under the civilising influence of Cathy and this will continue when he marries her and goes to live at Thrushcross Grange. Cathy was raised at the Grange and has her father's gentleness and decency, but the unpleasant social snobbery she also inherited is eradicated by her relationship with Hareton; moreover, she also possesses her mother's vitality and spirit, qualities which she shares with Hareton and which we associate with Wuthering Heights rather than Thrushcross Grange.

The justification for the second set of characters, then, is clear. What many critics have felt, however, is that these characters are less impressively realised than their predecessors, that the reader responds to them with reduced interest, sympathy and involvement. An examination of this argument might begin by considering the two most important characters of the second generation, Hareton and Cathy. Hareton is certainly sketchily drawn and for much of the novel is a peripheral figure. A fuller portrayal might have made more plausible his development from the brutal child who swears and throws stones at Nelly (and hangs a litter of puppies from a chairback) to the gentle, considerate youth of the final chapters. His affection for Heathcliff (an affection which is reciprocated) is convincingly represented, but his relationship with Cathy is of more importance to the novel and this will be considered shortly. Cathy is portrayed in greater detail and is more credible as a result. Nelly's account of her is undoubtedly partial ('She was the most winning thing that ever brought sunshine into a desolate house' — chapter 18), but this is offset by episodes illustrating less attractive aspects of her character (such as wilfulness and social snobbery) and by Lockwood's contrasting view: '"She does not seem so amiable", I thought, "as Mrs Dean would persuade me to believe. She's a beauty, it is true; but not an angel."' (chapter 31). By the end of the novel she has gained in maturity, and this is believable because the changes in her character arise naturally from her experiences and from the changes in her circumstances. She receives a sheltered upbringing at Thrushcross Grange and then endures a miserable, comfortless life at Wuthering Heights following her forced marriage to a sick, demanding husband. After Linton's death she becomes sullen and withdrawn before reaching out to Hareton for companionship and love.

The relationship that develops between Cathy and Hareton is, however, surely one of the weakest elements in the novel. It is important to the book's overall meaning that this relationship should appear more conventional, more 'normal' than that between Heathcliff and the elder Catherine. The latter relationship is shown to be unhealthily obsessive, destructive in its intensity and disregard for conventional moral standards. Cathy and Hareton's love, in contrast, is of a gentler, less dangerous kind and is approved of by Nelly and (or such would appear to be Emily Brontë's intention) by the reader. But the portrayal of a conventional love relationship carries with it the risk that the portrayal will itself appear conventional in the worst sense — trite, stereotyped, unoriginal. That Emily Brontë did not succeed in avoiding this trap is suggested by the contrast between the following two passages. In the first (taken from chapter 9) the elder Catherine, in conversation with Nelly, speaks of her feelings for Heathcliff; in the second (taken from chapter 32) Lockwood describes young Cathy teaching Hareton to read.

1   I cannot express it; but surely you and everybody have a notion that there is, or should be, an existence of yours beyond you. What were the use of my creation if I were entirely contained here? My great miseries in this world have been Heathcliff's miseries, and I watched and felt each from the beginning; my great thought in living is himself. If all else perished, and *he* remained, I should still continue to be; and if all else remained, and he were annihilated, the universe would turn to a mighty stranger. I should not seem a part of it. My love for Linton is like the foliage in the woods. Time will change it, I'm well aware, as winter changes the trees. My love for Heathcliff resembles the eternal rocks beneath — a source of little visible delight, but necessary. Nelly, I *am* Heathcliff — he's always, always in my mind — not as a pleasure, any more than I am always a pleasure to myself — but as my own being.

2   'Con-*trary!*' said a voice, as sweet as a silver bell — 'That for the third time, you dunce! I'm not going to tell you again. Recollect, or I pull your hair!'

      'Contrary, then,' answered another, in deep, but softened tones. 'And now, kiss me, for minding so well.'

      'No, read it over first correctly, without a single mistake.'

      The male speaker began to read — he was a young man, respectably dressed, and seated at a table, having a book before him. His handsome features glowed with pleasure, and his eyes kept impatiently wandering from the page to a small white hand over his shoulder, which recalled him by a smart slap on the cheek whenever its owner detected such signs of inattention.

      Its owner stood behind; her light shining ringlets blending at intervals with his brown locks, as she bent to superintend his studies . . .

In the first passage the extent of Catherine's love for Heathcliff is brought fully home to us by language which is vivid, direct and vigorous. The enduring nature of her feelings for Heathcliff and the superficiality of her love for Edgar are beautifully captured in the contrasting images of 'the foliage in the woods' and 'the eternal rocks beneath'. The emotions described are unusual, interesting and complex; the relationship with Heathcliff, for example, is based upon need rather than pleasure: 'a source of little visible delight, but necessary'. The second extract carries much less conviction. Whereas the first passage had originality and power, the description here draws too heavily on romantic cliché to achieve a similar impact: Cathy's voice is 'as sweet as a silver bell' and she has 'a small white hand' and 'light shining ringlets'; Hareton has 'handsome features' which 'glowed with pleasure'. Brontë's treatment of the Cathy–Hareton relationship is consistently marred by this kind of sentimentality and banality — other characteristic episodes are Hareton stroking Cathy's hair 'as gently as if it were a bird' (chapter 30) and Catherine sticking primroses in Hareton's porridge (chapter 33).

The third member of the second generation, Linton Heathcliff, embodies the worst traits of both the Linton family (physical and emotional weakness) and his father Heathcliff (selfishness and spite). However, he does so to such an extreme degree that he is rarely a believable character. His faults are so obvious that it seems implausible that Cathy should remain blind to them for so long. The novel suffers from a considerable loss of narrative interest in the chapters which describe Cathy and Linton's intermittent courtship and eventual marriage. Heathcliff's manipulation of the relationship is needlessly protracted (we first learn of his plan in chapter 21 and it is not fulfilled until chapter 27) and assisted by some unlikely coincidences (Cathy's chance meeting with Heathcliff in chapter 22, for example). It culminates in Cathy's kidnapping — a melodramatic and somewhat unconvincing episode.

It can of course be argued that the success of the second half of the novel is not entirely dependent upon the second generation of characters, as several members of the first generation outlive the elder Catherine. However, of the first generation characters who survive into the second half of the book, Hindley Earnshaw dies soon after Catherine, and Isabella Linton's death, though chronologically it occurs several years later, is reported in the same chapter (chapter 17). Hindley is a shadowy, rather unconvincing character after the death of his wife

Frances in chapter 8. A grotesquely dissipated figure ('his features were lost in masses of shaggy hair that hung on his shoulders' — chapter 13), he drinks and gambles his way to ruin. Isabella's character lacks complexity and her role in the novel is largely a passive one. She is one of Heathcliff's many victims and as such demonstrates the cruelty of his nature. Brontë presents her as a typical product of Thrushcross Grange: weak, snobbish and naïve. Marriage to Heathcliff toughens her; her decision to leave Heathcliff shows some spirit but after this she plays no further part in the novel.

Both characters are in any case secondary in importance to Catherine, Edgar and Heathcliff. Edgar is a more interesting character than his sister and demands a more complex response from the reader. He represents the conventional morality that means nothing to Heathcliff and Catherine: in Nelly's words, he is 'kind, and trustful, and honourable' (chapter 10). However, although he possesses genuine moral strength he also has an ineffectual, passionless nature that makes it impossible for him to satisfy Catherine's needs. There is subtlety and conviction in Brontë's portrayal of his character, but this portrayal is mostly to be found in the first half of the novel. After Catherine's death he becomes a background figure: he turns into a recluse, giving up his duties as magistrate and staying away from the village, and, though a doting father, remains ignorant of Heathcliff's manipulation of his daughter.

Heathcliff, of course, could never be described as a background figure. Although he withdraws briefly from the action following Hindley's death, he returns to dominate the novel. In the second half of the book we see the relentless execution of his revenge plan and, in the closing chapters, his growing conviction that he is about to be reunited with Catherine. The novel ends soon after Nelly has described his death. Any assessment of the artistic merit of the second half of the novel must be in large part an assessment of Emily Brontë's portrayal of Heathcliff in these later chapters. He is certainly a credible and sympathetic figure as a child; as the Victorian critic Mrs Humphry Ward observed, the early scenes have a 'marvellous and essential truth'. His hard, savage nature is understandable in view of his Liverpool slum background and the systematic degradation he suffers at the hands of Hindley after Mr Earnshaw's death. The development of his relationship with Catherine is also wholly believable: the two children have similar temperaments and Hindley's tyrannical regime strengthens their allegiance to each other. Heathcliff's distress, when Edgar — along with the world of wealth and privilege he represents — becomes a rival for Catherine's love, is movingly and convincingly rendered. When he returns after an absence of three years it is his malevolence which is consistently stressed. Soon after he reappears Nelly compares him to 'a bird of bad omen' and 'an evil beast . . . waiting his time to spring and destroy' (chapter 10). Whereas before he was a victim of the cruelty and callousness of others, he now inflicts suffering, causing Catherine's marriage to Edgar to disintegrate and exacting a brutal revenge upon the Earnshaw and Linton families. The fulfilment of this revenge occupies much of the second half of the novel: he encourages Hindley to destroy himself (at his funeral he wears an expression of 'flinty gratification at a piece of difficult work, successfully executed' — chapter 17), degrades Hareton, forces Cathy to marry Linton, and on Edgar's death seizes Thrushcross Grange. Many critics feel that Brontë's portrayal of Heathcliff the ruthless avenger is a much less impressive achievement than her account of his childhood. His brutality and his delight in his own savagery reach such extremes that at times he seems a monster rather than a credible human being — as when he hangs Isabella's puppy, or speaks of tearing out Edgar's heart and drinking his blood. Brontë's prose also suffers, with frequent lapses into melodrama, as illustrated by the following much-quoted passages:

> I have no pity! I have no pity! The more the worms writhe, the more I yearn to crush out their entrails!
>
> (chapter 14)

> His hair and clothes were whitened with snow, and his sharp cannibal teeth, revealed by cold and wrath, gleamed through the dark.
>
> (chapter 17)

In such passages Heathcliff has a satanic quality, and it is clear that in her portrayal of his character Brontë was influenced by the Gothic literature of her time. Tales of horror and the super-

natural were very much in fashion in the early part of the nineteenth century and characters possessed by the Devil were a
common feature. Nelly and Isabella both speak of Heathcliff as
a 'goblin'. Nelly also wonders if he is a 'ghoul, or a vampire',
while Isabella calls him a 'fiend' and describes his eyes as 'the
clouded windows of hell'. This conception of Heathcliff receives
its most grotesque corroboration when we hear of him opening
Catherine's coffin and gazing on her corpse. Defenders of Emily
Brontë argue that Heathcliff's behaviour reflects the extraordinary intensity of his passion, but it is difficult to refute Q D
Leavis's view that such episodes are a 'Gothic aberration'.

Heathcliff loses his desire for revenge in chapter 33 and in
what remains of the novel his character regains much of its
authority and conviction. Attention is focused not upon his
sadistic excesses but upon his agonised longing for Catherine,
and in place of the melodramatic ranting of earlier chapters
there are speeches of genuine emotional power:

> I cannot look down to this floor, but her features are shaped on
> the flags! In every cloud, in every tree — filling the air at night,
> and caught by glimpses in every object by day — I am
> surrounded with her image! The most ordinary faces of men, and
> women — my own features — mock me with a resemblance. The
> entire world is a dreadful collection of memoranda that she did
> exist, and that I have lost her!
>
> (chapter 33)

Equally affecting is his identification with Hareton, in whom he
can see 'the ghost of my immortal love, of my wild endeavours
to hold my right, my degradation, my pride, my happiness, and
my anguish' (chapter 33). The supernatural element in Heathcliff's belief that Catherine's spirit is still with him perhaps
receives too much emphasis, and the death itself is never plau-
sibly explained, but in general the description of Heathcliff's
last days is a memorable achievement and certainly over-
shadows the parallel story of Hareton and Cathy's love.

It is fitting that the novel should conclude by returning to
the relationship between Heathcliff and Catherine, for this is
where its chief interest lies. The love that develops between
Hareton and Cathy has some value as an interesting counter-
part to this relationship, but it is very much a subsidiary

in the novel and is clearly less of a creative success. The
nsibly ends on a note of harmony and tranquillity, with
and Cathy about to marry and Lockwood standing by
the graves of their predecessors wondering 'how anyone could
ever imagine unquiet slumbers for the sleepers in that quiet
earth'. But Catherine and Heathcliff's relationship has been
disturbing in its strength, intensity and disregard for convention, and the reports of the lovers' restlessly wandering ghosts
ensure that it continues to disturb, forcing us to question the
settled calm of the final paragraph. Most readers may stop short
of E M Forster's judgement that, 'Great as the novel is, one
cannot afterwards remember anything in it but Heathcliff and
the elder Catherine', but they are likely to agree that the book's
finest moments belong to these characters.

AFTERTHOUGHTS

What 'justification' does Gardiner offer for the 'second set' of characters (pages 88–89)?

Can you think of any reasons why Brontë should have given Catherine and her daughter the same Christian name?

Do you agree with Gardiner that 'the relationship between Cathy and Hareton is . . . one of the weakest elements in the novel' (page 90)?

What strengths and weaknesses does Gardiner identify in Brontë's portrayal of Heathcliff in the second half of the novel?

Stephen Jacobi

Stephen Jacobi teaches English at the United World College, Singapore.

ESSAY

The importance of not being Nelly: a structuralist approach

Most critics agree on the importance of Nelly Dean as the most significant narrator in *Wuthering Heights*. She shares this duty with Lockwood, Isabella, Cathy, Heathcliff and Zillah (who all weigh in to elaborate on what Nelly cannot know as well as they), but hers is undoubtedly the main single contribution, both in terms of the amount she has to say, and also the continuity and (supposed) objectivity she provides.

We are often urged to see Nelly in terms such as these: she is straightforward, honest, good-humoured and capable. Although she may hold traditional beliefs, her basic sense of humanity enables her to observe and judge the novel's events and characters in an entirely convincing way.

The viewpoint could be developed to state that Nelly's conventional morality throws the excesses of Heathcliff and Catherine into explicit relief, that her intellectual limitations lead to a simple trustworthiness, and that her position at Wuthering Heights (as a practical housekeeper and a curious woman) allows her to give a really concrete account of 'what happened'.

The main problem with all these views, quite sensible as they might seem, is that they depend on the reader reading the novel as if Nelly were a real person, and relying on her 'character' to give the right sort of information, guidance and perspective. Criticism of this kind often depends on the tension between Nelly's 'character' and the events she is describing, whereby a kind of sub-text is created, so that we settle on a 'meaning' which is suspended somewhere between what Nelly says was happening, and who Nelly actually is. Through her control of the reader's (often unconscious) responses to Nelly, Emily Brontë is able to maintain an artistic grip on narration and reaction. Such epithets as 'loyal', 'trustworthy', 'curious' and 'forthright' then come into their own as convincing evidence of Nelly's narrative credibility, and the reader obediently follows the clues to a logical conclusion.

However, this conclusion, or reading of the text, involves the formulation of ideas based upon expectations and assumptions which lie in the reader's conception of Nelly Dean's character. Rather than examining the text in detail, the reader will tend to be caught up in the general, misleading effect of Nelly's good humour, honesty, or whatever. The constructed character is therefore 'noticed' at the expense of important textual signals. This cosy, immensely practical and convenient reading of Nelly's character, and its effective contribution to *Wuthering Heights*, 'tempts', as Jonathan Culler puts it, readers into 'ignoring or reducing the strangeness of its (the text's) gaps and silences'.[1]

A structuralist reading of *Wuthering Heights* would oppose such conventional assumptions. Briefly (and simply), structuralism insists on the sanctity of text — that is, the potential of the linguistic codes, conventions and patterns within the text itself to explain and interpret themselves. The reader shouldn't have to draw on knowledge from 'outside' as an aid to understanding, for example, the constructed notion of a complete character called Nelly, whose presence would inevitably blur the clarity of the linguistic relations. The text explains and defines *itself*, and any other knowledge is deemed to be irrelevant. With

[1] Jonathan Culler, *Structuralist Poetics* (London, 1975), p.232.

the emphasis entirely on form, and the structure of the relations between the 'units' of the text, concepts such as 'character', and even 'meaning' become, to all intents and purposes, redundant.

At this point, it would be usual to start defining structuralism in terms of every unit (word) in language being a 'sign', mentioning some eminent linguists (e.g. Saussure), and discussing the crucial difference between each sign's components (i.e. the 'signifier' and the 'signified' — or, the physical shape and/or sound of the sign, contrasted with the actual image or concept summoned up by it). As these ideas have been more than adequately covered elsewhere, there seems to be little point in going over old ground. It is sufficient to say that, with this concentration on the text, or the words, structuralism simply examines the relations between the various words/items that it contains, and that the aim is not to uncover meaning, but only to identify differences and relationships in the language of the text. Structuralism therefore challenges the idea that art is related to life, and that characters in a novel, such as Nelly, can feed off the impression that they are identifiable in the outside world, and have an empirical distinctiveness. So, let us abandon the comfortable conception of 'Nelly', and analyse instead the signs and units of language which constitute 'her'.

The first time that the reader meets Nelly is through Lockwood, who is eager to hear the story that she can tell him. Just before she starts her narrative (chapter 4), Nelly and Lockwood exchange words, which help the reader to form an immediate impression of her — and will tend to mould the perceptions of her throughout the text. Consider these examples of Nelly's speech at this point:

> 'Why, sir, she is my late master's daughter: Catherine Linton was her maiden name. I nursed her, poor thing! I did wish Mr Heathcliff would remove here, and then we might have been together again.'

> 'Very old, sir; and Hareton is the last of them, as our Miss Cathy is of us — I mean, of the Lintons. Have you been to Wuthering Heights? I beg pardon for asking; but I should like to hear how she is.'

'Rough as a saw-edge, and hard as a whinstone! The less you meddle with him the better.'

(chapter 4)

This is Nelly's 'characteristic' tone. The vocabulary is simple, and the sentences are short, almost breathless, often broken by colons and semicolons, and containing both questions and exclamations. There is also a great sense of the 'personal' — the respectful repetition of 'sir', the colloquial phrasing and the willingness to give an opinion.

However, once Nelly begins her narration, the briefly established characteristic tone quickly becomes diluted, or combined with and punctuated by a series of other modes of narrative voice. A comparison of the different voices will clarify this. First, there is Nelly's mimetic mode (narration through the imitation of someone's speech, the characteristic tone already noted; that is, Nelly's narrative 'voice'), when she is lecturing Heathcliff after he has admitted crying during the night (chapter 7). The lucid certainty with which she utters the cliché which begins the lecture ('a proud heart and an empty stomach') indicates her reliance on the conventional, while much else of what she says is qualified by an appeal for support ('and that he does', 'I'll be bound', 'don't you feel that you could?'). In fact, the whole speech is tinged with a kind of aggressive nervousness (note the rhythm) that comes when Nelly moves away from the security of the cliché or the safe ground of homely advice. It is a type of discourse that is uniquely Nelly's.

Compare this to another moment of 'her' narration (when she is giving information, rather than reporting her own speech), when Master Linton inadvertently insults Heathcliff:

> ... but Heathcliff's violent nature was not prepared to endure the impertinence from one whom he seemed to hate, even then, as a rival. He seized a tureen of hot apple sauce, the first thing that came under his gripe, and dashed it full against the speaker's face and neck; who instantly commenced a lament that brought Isabella and Catherine hurrying to the place.

(chapter 7)

This passage occurs only two pages after the first example, but here the reader has an objectified, impersonal account of Heathcliff's character, not really in the accustomed manner of Nelly at all. The sentences are evenly balanced, with the punctuation being used to control the rhythm, rather than breaking it. There is also a deliberate coolness in the description of a dramatic incident, as if information was simply being imparted. Earlier, Nelly was promising to 'arrange' Heathcliff so that Edgar would only look like a 'doll' beside him. In this account though, the prejudice has been smoothed out, and the first sentence seems carefully to weigh the characters up ('violent nature' against 'impertinence'), while the use of the word 'lament' gives nothing away either.

So, whilst the reader might assume that Nelly's narrative is being handled mimetically (that is, her 'own' voice is heard throughout), a mildly structuralist approach shows that there are at least two different types of narration at work. The non-mimetic one tends to inform in a neutral manner, and doesn't provide the personalised tone and perspective the reader has been conditioned to assume is present.

One of the structuralist criticisms levelled at 'typical' nineteenth-century novels is that they rely too much on a single type of narration, whereby the authorial narration controls, interprets and judges all other styles, putting the reader in a position of considerable dominance over the characters and their stories. The argument goes that texts should refuse to privilege one discourse or style of narrative over another, and that the novel should be a tissue of discourses, all intermingling, never allowing the reader to be comfortable, and even being contradictory as well as diverse. I believe that this is what is happening in *Wuthering Heights*, and that far from writing a novel which comprises a number of purely mimetic narratives (of which Nelly's is the most significant), Emily Brontë does actually admit a proliferation of 'languages' into her text. That we read Nelly's narrative in terms of pre-established character is little more than a calculated illusion on the author's part, but once the layers are peeled away more carefully the 'character' of Nelly begins to dissolve into a number of related, but different, types of language.

I have already identified one of these types of language (or modes of discourse) as Nelly's 'mimetic mode', whilst the other, which is a more objective, evenly balanced voice, is the 'diegetic' mode. That is, anything that is not in dialogue, and is the impersonal report of the author-as-narrator. Further investigation would probably be able to place these narrative types more exactly — the mimetic might be used for imposing a conventional perspective, which often indulges Heathcliff and Cathy's story of passion, whereas the diegetic is very useful for imparting information, linking scenes and providing a cultural, social and environmental context. What is usually seen as the personalised story of a good-natured, practical woman — and derives a certain resonance from that — now fades into the rather less enchanting contrast of at least two narrative styles.

Nelly's 'disintegration' has often been noted, and the tension between her role as narrator and as an actor has been seen to make her a fairly unreliable narrator. There are further textual complications, though. Nelly's narrative is also corrupted by the intrusion of other characters' reported speeches, and also by what David Lodge has called 'free indirect speech'.[2] This is a device where the narrator fuses the mimetic and diegetic modes together, 'often indistinguishably and inextricably', by using an objectified narrative which is nevertheless 'coloured by the thoughts and feelings of a characer'.[3] This is neatly displayed in the following passage, where Mrs Linton is giving instructions to Nelly concerning a fit she is about to throw. She wishes it reported to her husband, so as to 'frighten' him:

> The stolidity with which I received these instructions was, no doubt, rather exasperating: for they were delivered in perfect sincerity; but I believed a person who could plan the turning of her fits of passion to account, beforehand, might, by exerting her will, manage to control herself tolerably, even while under their influence; and I did not wish to 'frighten' her husband, as she said, and multiply his annoyances for the purpose of serving her selfishness.
>
> (chapter 11)

---

[2] David Lodge, 'Middlemarch and the idea of the classic realistic text', in Arnold Kettle (ed.), *The Nineteenth Century Novel* (London, 1972), pp.225–226.
[3] Ibid., p.225.

Here, the reader can never be quite sure whether she is listening to Nelly's opinions, or the author's. The passage moves freely in and out of Nelly's consciousness; after starting with a third-person viewpoint of how her action might seem to others ('stolidity . . . exasperating'), it moves into the personal ('perfect sincerity' — only Nelly would have known this), before embarking on a sensible, apparently neutral and *common-sensical* opinion ('I believed . . .') and ending with a return to personal wilfulness ('I did not wish . . .'). The language is a combination of objective balance, pitted against the striving subjectivity of personal opinion, and the sense that this one, long sentence could trip over itself at any moment. It never does, but the suggestion is always present.

It is not the place of this essay to dwell on the literary influences at work in *Wuthering Heights*, but they do provide another narrative layer, and further complicate Nelly's story-telling. The matter has been dealt with elsewhere[4] and it is sufficient to say now that bits of Scott, the Gothic novel, Byron and Shakespeare found their ways into the text. Nelly herself implies this in an exchange with Lockwood:

> '. . . I have undergone sharp discipline, which has taught me wisdom: and then, I have read more than you would fancy, Mr Lockwood. You could not open a book in this library that I have not looked into, and got something out of . . .'

> (chapter 7)

As well as helping to substantiate the notion of literary borrowing, if this is accepted, then the statement might also contribute to the mimetic-diegetic confusion, where Nelly and the author are sometimes blurred together.

Finally, I wish to take a passage which draws together much of what I have been claiming, and makes the idea of narrative diversity (at the expense of clearly delineated character) quite explicit. Catherine has just announced her intention of marrying Linton, despite Nelly's criticism that this

---

[1] Most accessibly in Jacques Blondel's essay, 'Literary Influences on *Wuthering Heights*'; to be found in Miriam Allott (ed.), *Wuthering Heights* (Macmillan Casebooks, 1970).

would mean deserting Heathcliff, who, after supper, they are now looking for:

> I went and called, but got no answer. On returning, I whispered to Catherine that he had heard a good part of what she said, I was sure; and told how I saw him quit in the kitchen just as she complained of her brother's conduct regarding him. She jumped up in a fine fright, flung Hareton on to the settle, and ran to seek for her friend herself; not taking leisure to consider why she was so flurried, or how her talk would have affected him. She was absent such a while that Joseph proposed we should wait no longer. He cunningly conjectured that they were staying away in order to avoid hearing his protracted blessing. They were 'ill enough for only fahl manners,' he affirmed. And on their behalf he added that night a special prayer to the usual quarter of an hour's supplication before meat, and would have tacked another to the end of grace, had not his young mistress broken in upon him with a hurried command that he must run down the road, and wherever Heathcliff had rambled, find and make him re-enter directly!
>
> (chapter 9)

Here the reader is confronted with Nelly's own reported speech ('I whispered to Catherine that . . .'), her own colloquialisms ('I was sure', 'fine fright', 'quit'), and the initial bursts of action reported in active, bustling terms that could well have come from Nelly's restless lips ('jumped up', 'flung', 'ran'). Suddenly, however, there is a break from Nelly's sense of self, to a calmer, more authoratitive and meditative tone of voice; the reader is informed about the behaviour of the characters in a way that can only be described as distanced, judgemental and cool ('not taking leisure to consider why she was so flurried, or how her talk would have affected him') — in fact, in a way that takes it out of Nelly's consciousness. Joseph's linguistic idiosyncracies add a further diversion, before the passage moves into the last, long, breathless sentence that re-enacts Joseph's mistress's hurried speech rhythms, at Nelly's curious, eagerly rattling pace, but with the balance and relative control of the authorial voice. The final exclamation mark therefore provides a difficulty; who does it belong to? Does it replicate the mistress's attempt to impose urgency on Joseph, or Nelly's dramatic story-telling, or the author's amused, semi-ironic comment on the general hiatus that was ensuing?

The answer to this question is academic; the paragraph shows a variety of styles and modes of discourse, which confuse the distinction between 'showing and telling', mimesis and diegesis, in a complex and challenging manner. Maybe it is the difficulty of the text at such moments that persuades the reader to embrace the neatness of 'sense of character' even more tightly.

A structuralist view of *Wuthering Heights* therefore emphasises the general unease that the system has with the notion of character, and shows that Nelly's narrative, far from being an act of story-telling through the particularised eyes of a faithful retainer figure, is, in fact, a tangle of types of discourse, which often interfere and conflict with each other.

So what does it all prove? Well, although structuralism doesn't in itself provide 'themes', what it does do is provide a system of meaning within which texts may derive meaning. It identifies the linguistic structures that a particular text might employ, and then sorts those structures into a kind of pattern. The purpose of narrative is therefore to enact the terms of its presupposing system — a thematic viewpoint could then be held against this to see if it can be supported.

The theme of *Wuthering Heights* could be the magnificence of amoral passion, the value of excess and the heightened capacity for feeling. A structuralist could then argue that the opposition and conflict within Nelly's narrative therefore 'supports' the impression of a collision between two worlds (Wuthering Heights vs. Thrushcross Grange), and that the logic of the text has an opposition which underlines that given theme.

It is not the purpose of this essay to explore this idea any further, but merely to again emphasise that the invitation to see theme and narrative emerging through a reliable and loyal Nelly is a misguided one, and that she doesn't really exist as a consistent, empirical character at all.

AFTERTHOUGHTS

1

What are the problems of regarding Nelly's narrative as if she 'were a real person' (page 99)? Does this mean that the term 'character' can have no meaning for a structuralist reader?

2

What do you understand by 'sanctity of text' (page 99)?

3

Explain the relevance of Jacobi's description of Nelly's 'mimetic' and 'non-mimetic' modes of narration (pages 100–104) to his argument as a whole.

4

What can a consideration of a structuralist reading of *Wuthering Heights* add to your appreciation of the novel?

A PRACTICAL GUIDE TO ESSAY WRITING

INTRODUCTION

First, a word of warning. Good essays are the product of a creative engagement with literature. So never try to restrict your studies to what you think will be 'useful in the exam'. Ironically, you will restrict your grade potential if you do.

This doesn't mean, of course, that you should ignore the basic skills of essay writing. When you read critics, make a conscious effort to notice *how* they communicate their ideas. The guidelines that follow offer advice of a more explicit kind. But they are no substitute for practical experience. It is never easy to express ideas with clarity and precision. But the more often you tackle the problems involved and experiment to find your own voice, the more fluent you will become. So practise writing essays as often as possible.

HOW TO PLAN
AN ESSAY

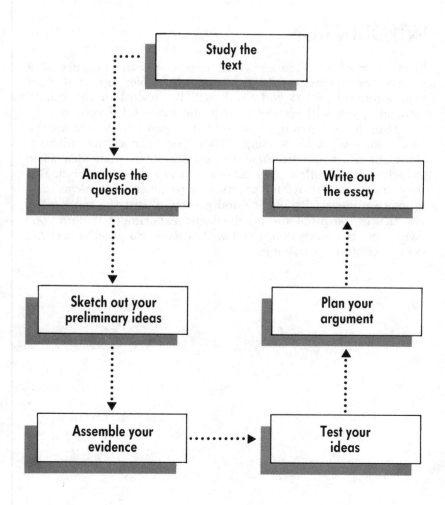

Study the text

The first step in writing a good essay is to get to know the set text well. Never write about a text until you are fully familiar with it. Even a discussion of the opening chapter of a novel, for example, should be informed by an understanding of the book as a whole. Literary texts, however, are by their very nature complex and on a first reading you are bound to miss many significant features. Re-read the book with care, if possible more than once. Look up any unfamiliar words in a good dictionary and if the text you are studying was written more than a few decades ago, consult the *Oxford English Dictionary* to find out whether the meanings of any terms have shifted in the intervening period.

Good books are difficult to put down when you first read them. But a more leisurely second or third reading gives you the opportunity to make notes on those features you find significant. An index of characters and events is often useful, particularly when studying novels with a complex plot or time scheme. The main aim, however, should be to record your *responses* to the text. By all means note, for example, striking images. But be sure to add *why* you think them striking. Similarly, record any thoughts you may have on interesting comparisons with other texts, puzzling points of characterisation, even what you take to be aesthetic blemishes. The important thing is to annotate fully and adventurously. The most seemingly idiosyncratic comment may later lead to a crucial area of discussion which you would otherwise have overlooked. It helps to have a working copy of the text in which to mark up key passages and jot down marginal comments (although obviously these practices are taboo when working with library, borrowed or valuable copies!). But keep a fuller set of notes as well and organise these under appropriate headings.

Literature does not exist in an aesthetic vacuum, how-ever, and you should try to find out as much as possible about the context of its production and reception. It is particu-larly important to read other works by the same author and writings by contemporaries. At this early stage, you may want to restrict your secondary reading to those standard reference works, such as biographies, which are widely available in public libraries. In the long run, however, it pays to read as wide a range of critical studies as possible.

Some students, and tutors, worry that such studies may stifle the development of any truly personal response. But this won't happen if you are alert to the danger and read critically. After all, you wouldn't passively accept what a stranger told you in conversation. The fact that a critic's views are in print does not necessarily make them any more authoritative (as a glance at the review pages of the *TLS* and *London Review of Books* will reveal). So question the views you find: 'Does this critic's interpretation agree with mine and where do we part company?' 'Can it be right to try and restrict this text's meanings to those found by its author or first audience?' 'Doesn't this passage treat a theatrical text as though it were a novel?' Often it is views which you reject which prove most valuable since they challenge you to articulate your own position with greater clarity. Be sure to keep careful notes on what the critic wrote, and your *reactions* to what the critic wrote.

Analyse the question

You cannot begin to answer a question until you understand what task it is you have been asked to perform. Recast the question in your own words and reconstruct the line of reasoning which lies behind it. Where there is a choice of topics, try to choose the one for which you are best prepared. It would, for example, be unwise to tackle 'How far do you agree that in *Paradise Lost* Milton transformed the epic models he inherited from ancient Greece and Rome?' without a working knowledge of Homer and Virgil (or *Paradise Lost* for that matter!). If you do not already know the works of these authors, the question should spur you on to read more widely — or discourage you from attempting it at all. The scope of an essay, however, is not always so obvious and you must remain alert to the implied demands of each question. How could you possibly 'Consider the view that *Wuthering Heights* transcends the conventions of the Gothic novel' without reference to at least some of those works which, the question suggests, have *not* transcended Gothic conventions?

When you have decided on a topic, analyse the terms of the question itself. Sometimes these self-evidently require careful definition: *tragedy* and *irony*, for example, are notoriously difficult concepts to pin down and you will probably need to consult a good dictionary of literary terms. Don't ignore, however, those seemingly innocuous phrases which often smuggle in significant assumptions. 'Does Macbeth lack the nobility of the true tragic hero?' obviously invites you to discuss nobility and the nature of the tragic hero. But what of 'lack' and 'true' — do they suggest that the play would be improved had Shakespeare depicted Macbeth in a different manner? or that tragedy is superior to other forms of drama? Remember that you are not expected meekly to agree with the assumptions implicit in the question. Some questions are deliberately provocative in order to stimulate an engaged response. Don't be afraid to take up the challenge.

Sketch out your preliminary ideas

'Which comes first, the evidence or the answer?' is one of those chicken and egg questions. How can you form a view without inspecting the evidence? But how can you know which evidence is relevant without some idea of what it is you are looking for? In practice the mind reviews evidence and formulates preliminary theories or hypotheses at one and the same time, although for the sake of clarity we have separated out the processes. Remember that these early ideas are only there to get you started. You *expect* to modify them in the light of the evidence you uncover. Your initial hypothesis may be an instinctive 'gut-reaction'. Or you may find that you prefer to 'sleep on the problem', allowing ideas to gell over a period of time. Don't worry in either case. The mind is quite capable of processing a vast amount of accumulated evidence, the product of previous reading and thought, and reaching sophisticated intuitive judgements. Eventually, however, you are going to have to think carefully through any ideas you arrive at by such intuitive processes. Are they logical? Do they take account of all the relevant factors? Do they fully answer the question set? Are there any obvious reasons to qualify or abandon them?

Assemble your evidence

Now is the time to return to the text and re-read it with the question and your working hypothesis firmly in mind. Many of the notes you have already made are likely to be useful, but assess the precise relevance of this material and make notes on any new evidence you discover. The important thing is to cast your net widely and take into account points which tend to undermine your case as well as those that support it. As always, ensure that your notes are full, accurate, and reflect your own critical judgements.

You may well need to go outside the text if you are to do full justice to the question. If you think that the 'Oedipus complex' may be relevant to an answer on *Hamlet* then read Freud and a balanced selection of those critics who have discussed the appropriateness of applying psychoanalytical theories to the interpretation of literature. Their views can most easily be tracked down by consulting the annotated bibliographies held by most major libraries (and don't be afraid to ask a librarian for help in finding and using these). Remember that you go to works of criticism not only to obtain information but to stimulate you into clarifying your own position. And that since life is short and many critical studies are long, judicious use of a book's index and/or contents list is not to be scorned. You can save yourself a great deal of future labour if you carefully record full bibliographic details at this stage.

Once you have collected the evidence, organise it coherently. Sort the detailed points into related groups and identify the quotations which support these. You must also assess the relative importance of each point, for in an essay of limited length it is essential to establish a firm set of priorities, exploring some ideas in depth while discarding or subordinating others.

Test your ideas

As we stressed earlier, a hypothesis is only a proposal, and one that you fully expect to modify. Review it with the evidence before you. Do you really still believe in it? It would be surprising if you did not want to modify it in some way. If you cannot see any problems, others may. Try discussing your ideas with friends and relatives. Raise them in class discussions. Your tutor is certain to welcome your initiative. The critical process is essentially collaborative and there is absolutely no reason why you should not listen to and benefit from the views of others. Similarly, you should feel free to test your ideas against the theories put forward in academic journals and books. But do not just borrow what you find. Critically analyse the views on offer and, where appropriate, integrate them into your own pattern of thought. You must, of course, give full acknowledgement to the sources of such views.

Do not despair if you find you have to abandon or modify significantly your initial position. The fact that you are prepared to do so is a mark of intellectual integrity. Dogmatism is never an academic virtue and many of the best essays explore the *process* of scholarly enquiry rather than simply record its results.

Plan your argument

Once you have more or less decided on your attitude to the question (for an answer is never really 'finalised') you have to present your case in the most persuasive manner. In order to do this you must avoid meandering from point to point and instead produce an organised argument — a structured flow of ideas and supporting evidence, leading logically to a conclusion which fully answers the question. Never begin to write until you have produced an outline of your argument.

You may find it easiest to begin by sketching out its main stage as a flow chart or some other form of visual presentation. But eventually you should produce a list of paragraph topics. The paragraph is the conventional written demarcation for a unit of thought and you can outline an argument quite simply by briefly summarising the substance of each paragraph and then checking that these points (you may remember your English teacher referring to them as topic sentences) really do follow a coherent order. Later you will be able to elaborate on each topic, illustrating and qualifying it as you go along. But you will find this far easier to do if you possess from the outset a clear map of where you are heading.

All questions require some form of an argument. Even so-called 'descriptive' questions *imply* the need for an argument. An adequate answer to the request to 'Outline the role of Iago in *Othello*' would do far more than simply list his appearances on stage. It would at the very least attempt to provide some *explanation* for his actions — is he, for example, a representative stage 'Machiavel'? an example of pure evil, 'motiveless malignity'? or a realistic study of a tormented personality reacting to identifiable social and psychological pressures?

Your conclusion ought to address the terms of the question. It may seem obvious, but 'how far do you agree', 'evaluate', 'consider', 'discuss', etc, are *not* interchangeable formulas and your conclusion must take account of the precise wording of the question. If asked 'How far do you agree?', the concluding paragraph of your essay really should state whether you are in complete agreement, total disagreement, or, more likely, partial agreement. Each preceding paragraph should have a clear justification for its existence and help to clarify the reasoning which underlies your conclusion. If you find that a paragraph serves no good purpose (perhaps merely summarising the plot), do not hesitate to discard it.

The arrangement of the paragraphs, the overall strategy of the argument, can vary. One possible pattern is dialectical: present the arguments in favour of one point of view (**thesis**); then turn to counter-arguments or to a rival interpretation (**antithesis**); finally evaluate the competing claims and arrive at your own conclusion (**synthesis**). You may, on the other hand, feel so convinced of the merits of one particular case that you wish to devote your entire essay to arguing that viewpoint persuasively (although it is always desirable to indicate, however briefly, that you are aware of alternative, if flawed, positions). As the essays contained in this volume demonstrate, there are many other possible strategies. Try to adopt the one which will most comfortably accommodate the demands of the question and allow you to express your thoughts with the greatest possible clarity.

Be careful, however, not to apply abstract formulas in a mechanical manner. It is true that you should be careful to define your terms. It is *not* true that every essay should begin with 'The dictionary defines x as . . .'. In fact, definitions are often best left until an appropriate moment for their introduction arrives. Similarly every essay should have a beginning, middle and end. But it does not follow that in your opening paragraph you should announce an intention to write an essay, or that in your concluding paragraph you need to signal an imminent desire to put down your pen. The old adages are often useful reminders of what constitutes good practice, but they must be interpreted intelligently.

Write out the essay

Once you have developed a coherent argument you should aim to communicate it in the most effective manner possible. Make certain you clearly identify yourself, and the question you are answering. Ideally, type your answer, or at least ensure your handwriting is legible and that you leave sufficient space for your tutor's comments. Careless presentation merely distracts from the force of your argument. Errors of grammar, syntax and spelling are far more serious. At best they are an irritating blemish, particularly in the work of a student who should be sensitive to the nuances of language. At worst, they seriously confuse the sense of your argument. If you are aware that you have stylistic problems of this kind, ask your tutor for advice at the earliest opportunity. Everyone, however, is liable to commit the occasional howler. The only remedy is to give yourself plenty of time in which to proof-read your manuscript (often reading it aloud is helpful) before submitting it.

Language, however, is not only an instrument of communication; it is also an instrument of thought. If you want to think clearly and precisely you should strive for a clear, precise prose style. Keep your sentences short and direct. Use modern, straightforward English wherever possible. Avoid repetition, clichés and wordiness. Beware of generalisations, simplifications, and overstatements. Orwell analysed the relationship between stylistic vice and muddled thought in his essay 'Politics and the English Language' (1946) — it remains essential reading (and is still readily available in volume 4 of the Penguin *Collected Essays, Journalism and Letters*). Generalisations, for example, are always dangerous. They are rarely true and tend to suppress the individuality of the texts in question. A remark such as 'Keats always employs sensuous language in his poetry' is not only fatuous (what, after all, does it mean? is *every* word he wrote equally 'sensuous'?) but tends to obscure interesting distinctions which could otherwise be made between, say, the descriptions in the 'Ode on a Grecian Urn' and those in 'To Autumn'.

The intelligent use of quotations can help you make your points with greater clarity. Don't sprinkle them throughout your essay without good reason. There is no need, for example, to use them to support uncontentious statements of fact. 'Macbeth murdered Duncan' does not require textual evidence (unless you wish to dispute Thurber's brilliant parody, 'The Great Macbeth Murder Mystery', which reveals Lady Macbeth's father as the culprit!). Quotations should be included, however, when they are necessary to support your case. The proposition that Macbeth's imaginative powers wither after he has killed his king would certainly require extensive quotation: you would almost certainly want to analyse key passages from both before and after the murder (perhaps his first and last soliloquies?). The key word here is 'analyse'. Quotations cannot make your points on their own. It is up to you to demonstrate their relevance and clearly explain to your readers *why* you want them to focus on the passage you have selected.

Most of the academic conventions which govern the presentation of essays are set out briefly in the style sheet below. The question of gender, however, requires fuller discussion. More than half the population of the world is female. Yet many writers still refer to an undifferentiated *man*kind. Or write of the author and *his* public. We do not think that this convention has much to recommend it. At the very least, it runs the risk of introducing unintended sexist attitudes. And at times leads to such patent absurdities as 'Cleopatra's final speech asserts *man*'s true nobility'. With a little thought, you can normally find ways of expressing yourself which do not suggest that the typical author, critic or reader is male. Often you can simply use plural forms, which is probably a more elegant solution than relying on such awkward formulations as 's/he' or 'he and she'. You should also try to avoid distinguishing between male and female authors on the basis of forenames. Why *Jane* Austen and not *George* Byron? Refer to all authors by their last names unless there is some good reason not to. Where there may otherwise be confusion, say between T S and George Eliot, give the name in full when it first occurs and thereafter use the last name only.

Finally, keep your audience firmly in mind. Tutors and examiners are interested in understanding your conclusions and the processes by which you arrived at them. They are not interested in reading a potted version of a book they already know. **So don't pad out your work with plot summary.**

Hints for examinations

In an examination you should go through exactly the same processes as you would for the preparation of a term essay. The only difference lies in the fact that some of the stages will have had to take place before you enter the examination room. This should not bother you unduly. Examiners are bound to avoid the merely eccentric when they come to formulate papers and if you have read widely and thought deeply about the central issues raised by your set texts you can be confident you will have sufficient material to answer the majority of questions sensibly.

The fact that examinations impose strict time limits makes it *more* rather than less, important that you plan carefully. There really is no point in floundering into an answer without any idea of where you are going, particularly when there will not be time to recover from the initial error.

Before you begin to answer any question at all, study the entire paper with care. Check that you understand the rubric and know how many questions you have to answer and whether any are compulsory. It may be comforting to spot a title you feel confident of answering well, but don't rush to tackle it: read *all* the questions before deciding which *combination* will allow you to display your abilities to the fullest advantage. Once you have made your choice, analyse each question, sketch out your ideas, assemble the evidence, review your initial hypothesis, play your argument, *before* trying to write out an answer. And make notes at each stage: not only will these help you arrive at a sensible conclusion, but examiners are impressed by evidence of careful thought.

Plan your time as well as your answers. If you have practised writing timed essays as part of your revision, you should not find this too difficult. There can be a temptation to allocate extra time to the questions you know you can answer well; but this is always a short-sighted policy. You will find yourself left to face a question which would in any event have given you difficulty without even the time to give it serious thought. It is, moreover, easier to gain marks at the lower end of the scale than at the upper, and you will never compensate for one poor answer by further polishing two satisfactory answers. Try to leave some time at the end of the examination to re-read your answers and correct any obvious errors. If the worst comes to the worst and you run short of time, don't just keep writing until you are forced to break off in mid-paragraph. It is far better to provide for the examiner a set of notes which indicate the overall direction of your argument.

Good luck — but if you prepare for the examination conscientiously and tackle the paper in a methodical manner, you won't need it!

STYLE SHEET

book title in italics.
In a handwritten or
typed manuscript this
would appear as underlining:
Wuthering Heights.

Page references or
chapter references should
be given in assignment
essays and in examination
essays where a text
is supplied.

Three dots (ellipsis)
indicate where words
or phrases have been
cut from a quotation.

long prose quotation.
indented and introduced
by a colon. Quotation
marks are not required.

Short prose quotations
incorporated in the text
of the essay, within
quotation marks.

above the ground' (chapter 22). Although the polarised view of
Wuthering Heights and Thrushcross Grange is crucial to the plot
of the novel and helps to express the theme of Catherine's
betrayal, Nelly's more accommodating view is important. She
can see happiness in both localities. In fact the landscape of the
moors is, in *Wuthering Heights*, much more sweet than harsh.
It is bleak and repellent at first, answering Lockwood's preconceived romantic notions of what is proper to the rural desolation
of a 'misanthropist's heaven' (chapter 1). But more often the
moors are balmy, blooming and full of birdsong:

> The sky is blue and the larks are singing, and the becks and
> brooks are all brim full . . . I wish you were a mile or two up
> those hills: the air blows so sweetly . . .
>
> (chapter 1)

This lyrical description is by Edgar Linton. Edgar, of course,
comes to love the moors because he loves Catherine. Lockwood's
vision also develops. This is his final description as he looks at
the three graves on the edge of the moor:

> I lingered round them, under that benign sky: watched the
> moths fluttering among the heath and harebells; listened to the
> soft wind breathing through the grass.
>
> (chapter 34)

The graves are the end of a story that really begins in a bed
— the panelled bed in which Lockwood has his terrible
encounter with the spirit of Catherine. Both bed and grave are
fashioned for resting; they are uncannily parallel places. At the
height of her second fever (chapter 12), Catherine is haunted by
an image: 'I thought I was at home . . . I thought I was lying
in my bed at Wuthering Heights' and again 'Oh, if I were but
in my own bed in the old house! . . . And the wind sounding in
the firs by the lattice'. To the reader, perhaps sharing Lockwood's original experience in the chamber, it seems eery and
disturbing; and in fact Catherine's own associations are not
really of comfort. She relates her delirious conviction 'that I was
enclosed in the oak-panelled bed at home; and my heart ached
with some great grief which, just waking, I could not recollect'.
Then she identifies the grief of seven years previously: 'My
misery arose from the separation that Hindley had ordered

26

121

We have divided the following information into two sections. Part A describes those rules which it is essential to master no matter what kind of essay you are writing (including examination answers). Part B sets out some of the more detailed conventions which govern the documentation of essays.

PART A: LAYOUT

Titles of texts

Titles of published books, plays (of any length), long poems, pamphlets and periodicals (including newspapers and magazines), works of classical literature, and films should be underlined: e.g. David Copperfield (novel), Twelfth Night (play), Paradise Lost (long poem), Critical Quarterly (periodical), Horace's Ars Poetica (Classical work), Apocalypse Now (film).

Notice how important it is to distinguish between titles and other names. Hamlet is the play; Hamlet the prince. Wuthering Heights is the novel; Wuthering Heights the house. Underlining is the equivalent in handwritten or typed manuscripts of printed italics. So what normally appears in this volume as *Othello* would be written as Othello in your essay.

Titles of articles, essays, short stories, short poems, songs, chapters of books, speeches, and newspaper articles are enclosed in quotation marks; e.g. 'The Flea' (short poem), 'The Prussian Officer' (short story), 'Middleton's Chess Strategies' (article), 'Thatcher Defects!' (newspaper headline).

Exceptions: Underlining titles or placing them within quotation marks does not apply to sacred writings (e.g. Bible, Koran, Old Testament, Gospels) or parts of a book (e.g. Preface, Introduction, Appendix).

It is generally incorrect to place quotation marks around a title of a published book which you have underlined. The exception is 'titles within titles': e.g. 'Vanity Fair': A Critical Study (title of a book about *Vanity Fair*).

Quotations

Short verse quotations of a single line or part of a line should be incorporated within quotation marks as part of the running text of your essay. Quotations of two or three lines of verse are treated in the same way, with line endings indicated by a slash(/). For example:

1   In <u>Julius Caesar</u>, Antony says of Brutus, 'This was the noblest Roman of them all'.
2   The opening of Antony's famous funeral oration, 'Friends, Romans, Countrymen, lend me your ears;/ I come to bury Caesar not to praise him', is a carefully controlled piece of rhetoric.

Longer verse quotations of more than three lines should be indented from the main body of the text and introduced in most cases with a colon. Do not enclose indented quotations within quotation marks. For example:

It is worth pausing to consider the reasons Brutus gives to justify his decision to assassinate Caesar:

> It must be by his death; and for my part,
> I know no personal cause to spurn at him,
> But for the general. He would be crowned.
> How might that change his nature, there's the question.

At first glance his rationale may appear logical . . .

Prose quotations of less than three lines should be incorporated in the text of the essay, within quotation marks. Longer prose quotations should be indented and the quotation marks omitted. For example:

1   Before his downfall, Caesar rules with an iron hand. His political opponents, the Tribunes Marullus and Flavius, are 'put to silence' for the trivial offence of 'pulling scarfs off Caesar's image'.
2   It is interesting to note the rhetorical structure of Brutus's Forum speech:

> Romans, countrymen, and lovers, hear me for my cause, and be silent that you may hear. Believe me for my honour, and have respect to mine honour that you may believe. Censure me in your wisdom, and awake your senses, that you may the better judge.

Tenses: When you are relating the events that occur within a work of fiction, or describing the author's technique, it is the convention to use the present tense. Even though Orwell published *Animal Farm* in 1945, the book *describes* the animals' seizure of Manor Farm. Similarly, Macbeth always *murders* Duncan, despite the passage of time.

PART B: DOCUMENTATION

When quoting from verse of more than twenty lines, provide line references: e.g. In 'Upon Appleton House' Marvell's mower moves 'With whistling scythe and elbow strong' (l.393).

Quotations from plays should be identified by act, scene and line references: e.g. Prospero, in Shakespeare's The Tempest, refers to Caliban as 'A devil, a born devil' (IV.1.188). (i.e. Act 4. Scene 1. Line 188).

Quotations from prose works should provide a chapter reference and, where appropriate, a page reference.

Bibliographies should list full details of all sources consulted. The way is which they are presented varies, but one standard format is as follows:

1 Books and articles are listed in alphabetical order by the author's last name. Initials are placed after the surname.
2 If you are referring to a chapter or article within a larger work, you list it by reference to the author of the article or chapter, not the editor (although the editor is also named in the reference).
3 Give (in parentheses) the place and date of publication, e.g. (London, 1962). These details can be found within the book itself. Here are some examples:

> Brockbank, J. P., 'Shakespeare's Histories, English and Roman', in Ricks, C. (ed.) English Drama to 1710 (Sphere History of Literature in the English Language) (London, 1971).
> Gurr, A., 'Richard III and the Democratic Process', Essays in Criticism 24 (1974), pp. 39–47.
> Spivack, B., Shakespeare and the Allegory of Evil (New York, 1958).

Footnotes: In general, try to avoid using footnotes and build your references into the body of the essay wherever possible. When you do use them give the full bibliographic reference to a work in the first instance and then use a short title: e.g. See K. Smidt, <u>Unconformities in Shakespeare's History Plays</u> (London, 1982), pp. 43–47 becomes Smidt (pp. 43–47) thereafter. Do not use terms such as 'ibid.' or 'op. cit.' unless you are absolutely sure of their meaning.

There is a principle behind all this seeming pedantry. The reader ought to be able to find and check your references and quotations as quickly and easily as possible. Give additional information, such as canto or volume number whenever you think it will assist your reader.

SUGGESTIONS FOR FURTHER READING

Other works by Emily Brontë

A selection of Emily Brontë's poetry can be found in:

Davies, S, *The Brontë Sisters: Selected Poems* (Manchester, 1976)

Biography

Chitham, E, *A Life of Emily Brontë* (Oxford, 1987)

Gerin, W, *Emily Brontë* (Oxford, 1971)

Studies of works by Emily Brontë

Davies, S, *Emily Brontë: The Artist as a Free Woman* (Manchester, 1983)

Hardy, B, *Wuthering Heights* (Blackwell Notes on English Literature, 1963)

Holderness, G, *Wuthering Heights* (Milton Keynes, 1985)

Essay collections containing essays on *Wuthering Heights*

Allott, M (ed.), *Emily Brontë's 'Wuthering Heights'* (Macmillan Casebooks, 1970)

Gregor, I (ed.), *Twentieth Century Views: The Brontës* (Englewood Cliffs, NJ, 1970)

Lane, M, *The Drug-like Brontë Dream* (London, 1980)

Longman Group Limited
*Longman House, Burnt Mill, Harlow, Essex, CM20 2JE, England
and Associated Companies throughout the World.*

First published 1988
Fourth impression 1994
ISBN 0 582 00654 6

*Set in 10 / 12pt Century Schoolbook, Linotron 202
Produced through Longman Malaysia, GPS*

Acknowledgement
The editors would like to thank Zachary Leader for his assistance
with the style sheet.

The Publisher's policy is to use paper manufactured from
sustainable forests.